KS2 COMPREHENSION SATs SUCCESS TOPIC WORKBOOK

Ages 7–9

KS2
COMPREHENSION
SATs
TOPIC
WORKBOOK

RACHEL AXTEN-HIGGS

About this book

Comprehension

Ensuring children can read with good understanding is one of the main aims of the new primary curriculum. This book helps to improve comprehension skills across fiction, plays, poetry and non-fiction, breaking down each of these genres into easy-to-digest topics. Each topic is introduced by concise explanations and is explored through a variety of extract-based activities and questions. The test-style questions aid preparation for the **Reading** paper in the Key Stage 2 National Curriculum Tests (also known as SATs).

Features of the book

Key to comprehension provides concise explanations of the key concepts.

Comprehension material helps to explore each skill with an appropriate text, upon which *Practice activities* and *Test-style questions* are set.

Practice activities are designed to specifically help your child to understand the concept introduced in *Key to comprehension.*

Test-style questions help to build wider comprehension skills with questions reflecting those in the Key Stage 2 Reading National Curriculum Test.

Top tips give helpful hints to your child as they read and work through the topics.

Answers are in a pull-out booklet at the centre of the book.

Your child should keep referring to the extract while attempting the activities and questions. If they need more space to write an answer, encourage them to continue on a separate sheet of paper.

Comprehension tips

- Regular practice (10–15 minutes every day) will help your child to improve their reading. Take them to the library to let them discover different books and new authors. Reading a wide variety of books will keep it exciting and fun.
- Let your child read without distractions and only when they are relaxed and happy. Books can take them into new worlds and new experiences.
- Encourage your child to think about the text as they are reading. Does it make sense? If not, why not? It may be that they have misread a word and need to go back and correct themselves.
- Ask your child to read a particular page of a book and give them questions about it to test their understanding of the text.

When preparing for a reading test, remind your child to read the text **carefully**, read the question **carefully** and answer the question **using the text**. When asked, they should provide **evidence** from the text to back up their answer. Encourage them to **check** that they have fully answered the question.

Contents

What are classic stories?

Key to comprehension

Classic stories are well-known stories that are timeless. They were often written many years ago but are still enjoyed today.

For instance, because they are so popular, the Harry Potter books may withstand the test of time and become classic stories many years from now.

Classic stories may have old-fashioned language and references to items that are no longer in use today.

Top tip

Look at the imprint page at the beginning or end of a book to find the date it was first published.

Comprehension material

Extract from *Swallows and Amazons* by Arthur Ransome

Roger, aged seven, and no longer the youngest of the family, ran in wide zigzags, to and fro, across the steep field that sloped up from the lake to Holly Howe, the farm where they were staying for part of the summer holidays. He ran until he nearly reached the hedge by the footpath, then turned and ran until he nearly reached the hedge on the other side of the field. Then he turned and crossed the field again. Each crossing of the field brought him nearer to the farm. The wind was against him, and he was tacking up against it to the farm, where at the gate his patient mother was awaiting him. He could not run straight against the wind because he was a sailing vessel, a tea-clipper, the *Cutty Sark*. His elder brother John had said only that morning that steamships were just engines in tin boxes. Sail was the thing, and so, though it took rather longer, Roger made his way up the field in broad tacks.

When he came near his mother, he saw that she had in her hand a red envelope and a small piece of white paper, a telegram.

Practice activities

1. Why is this book a classic?

Tick **one**

It was written recently. ☐

It was written some time ago and is still read today. ☐

It is a fun story to read. ☐

2. What old-fashioned form of communication is mentioned in the text?

____

Test-style questions

1. How old is Roger? Circle **one** answer.

10 **8** **7** **9** *1 mark*

2. What time of year is it? Circle **one** answer.

autumn **summer** **winter** **spring** *1 mark*

3. Why was Roger running in a zigzag across the field?

____

____

2 marks

4. Write the missing words in this description.

...the steep field that sloped up from the _____________ to _____________

2 marks

5. Find and copy the phrase John uses to describe steamships.

____

1 mark

Themes in classic stories

Key to comprehension

A **theme** is an idea in a text – an idea the author wants you to think about. The author doesn't tell you what the theme is. You have to figure it out for yourself from what happens, what the characters do and what they say.

Some themes are found in many books. For example:

- good and evil
- rags to riches
- rewards for good deeds.

Top tip

Learn some of the universal themes as they are common to many stories.

Comprehension material

Extract from *The Wind in the Willows* by Kenneth Grahame

The Badger drew himself up, took a firm grip of his stick with both paws, glanced round at his comrades, and cried:

"The hour is come! Follow me!"

And flung the door open wide.

My!

What a squealing and a squeaking and a screeching filled the air!

Well might the terrified weasels dive under the tables and spring madly up at the windows! Well might the ferrets rush wildly for the fire-place and get hopelessly jammed in the chimney! Well might tables and chairs be upset, and glass and china be sent crashing on the floor, in the panic of that terrible moment when the four Heroes strode wrathfully into the room! The mighty Badger, his whiskers bristling, his great cudgel whistling through the air; Mole, black and grim, brandishing his stick and shouting his awful war-cry, "A Mole! A Mole!" Rat, desperate and determined, his belt bulging with weapons of every age and every variety; Toad, frenzied with excitement and injured pride, swollen to twice his ordinary size, leaping into the air and emitting Toad-whoops that chilled them to the marrow!

…

The affair was soon over. Up and down, the whole length of the hall, strode the four Friends, whacking with their sticks at every head that showed itself; and in five minutes the room was cleared.

Practice activities

1. Who are the four "Heroes"?

____

2. What animals were the Heroes fighting?

____

Test-style questions

1. One of the characters is described as "desperate and determined". Circle the character to whom this refers.

Rat **Mole** **Toad** **Badger** *1 mark*

2. What was Badger carrying when he entered?

____________________ *1 mark*

3. Where does the action take place?

	Tick **one**
outside	☐
on the river	☐
in a hall	☐
in the wild wood	☐

1 mark

4. What verb is used to show how the weasels got under the table?

____________________ *1 mark*

Words in context

Key to comprehension

Authors work hard to make their writing exciting for readers by using words and phrases in different ways.

Sometimes, a word that you know well might be used to mean something different from its literal meaning; to understand its meaning you must look at the context in which it is used.

When reading, you must continually check your understanding of words that are unfamiliar or used in a different way.

Top tip

When reading, use a dictionary to look up the meaning of words you don't know.

Comprehension material

Extract from *Peter Pan* by J. M. Barrie

A moment after the fairy's entrance the window was blown open by the breathing of the little stars, and Peter dropped in. He had carried Tinker Bell part of the way, and his hand was still messy with the fairy dust.

"Tinker Bell," he called softly, after making sure that the children were asleep, "Tink, where are you?" She was in a jug for the moment, and liking it extremely; she had never been in a jug before.

"Oh, do come out of that jug, and tell me, do you know where they put my shadow?"

The loveliest tinkle as of golden bells answered him. It is the fairy language. You ordinary children can never hear it, but if you were to hear it you would know that you had heard it once before.

Tink said that the shadow was in the big box. She meant the chest of drawers, and Peter jumped at the drawers, scattering their contents to the floor with both hands, as kings toss ha'pence to the crowd. In a moment he had recovered his shadow, and in his delight he forgot that he had shut Tinker Bell up in the drawer.

Practice activities

1. The word "softly" in the phrase "he called softly", is not used to mean something that is soft to the touch.

What does it mean in this context?

____

2. The window is said to have been "blown open by the breathing of the little stars".

What do you think might have really blown the window open?

____

Test-style questions

1. What is Tinker Bell? Circle **one** answer.

a little girl **a doll** **a fairy** **a shadow** *1 mark*

2. What can ordinary children never hear? Circle **one** answer.

golden bells **fairy language** **crying** **stars** *1 mark*

3. The words "Peter dropped in" do not mean that he has been dropped by somebody.

What do they mean?

____

____

2 marks

4. What does Tinker Bell call the chest of drawers?

____

1 mark

Key to comprehension

A **fairy tale** is a short story that usually features magic and fantasy characters, for example, talking animals, fairies, giants and elves.

The typical **structure** of a fairy tale is that a bad character is defeated / changed / made good and the good characters live happily ever after.

Comprehension material

The Frog Prince

Once upon a time there lived a very spoilt princess. One day she took her golden ball into the woods. As she walked she threw the ball up into the air, and, on the third throw, the ball rolled into a deep well. She shouted and kicked the well but with no luck. She was just about to kick the well again when a frog plopped out from it.

"Yuck," said the princess.

"What are you making such a noise and fuss about?" asked the frog.

The princess was speechless; a talking frog! It didn't take long for her to recover and she told the frog about her lost ball and how she wanted it back. The frog jumped in and retrieved it. The princess went to snatch it from him, but the frog told her to ask for it nicely; reluctantly she did. Before the frog gave the ball to the princess he told her that, in return, he wanted to live with her in the palace, eat from her plate and sleep on her pillow. The princess was not happy but wanted her ball back, so she agreed (thinking that a promise to a frog wouldn't matter). She went back to the palace with her ball.

That evening, when the family sat down to eat, they heard a voice – it was the frog asking for the princess. She had to explain to her parents what had happened, and they told her that she had to keep her promise. So, the frog sat next to her at the table (she did not eat a thing). He slept on the bed with her (she did not sleep a wink). This happened again on the second day.

By the third day, the princess was so hungry she ate from her plate. She was so tired, she slept through the night. On the morning of the fourth day she woke up and looked for the frog. He was not there. Standing at the foot of her bed, however, was a handsome prince.

"Who are you?" she screamed.

"I was the frog who rescued your golden ball. I was bewitched by a fairy who told me I was rude and spoilt. She said the spell could only be broken by someone equally rude and spoilt having to be nice to me…so, here I am!"

Practice activities

1. What are the magical features of the story? Write down **two**.

2. The princess could be described as the bad and the good character in the story.

   What evidence is there that she was bad?

Test-style questions

1. Who told the princess she had to keep her promise? Circle **one** answer.

   the frog **herself** **her parents** **the fairy** *1 mark*

2. Why was the princess speechless when she met the frog?

   1 mark

3. Why do you think the princess did not eat anything on the first and second days?

   2 marks

4. What do you think the prince's experience taught him about how to treat people?

   1 mark

The language of fairy tales

Key to comprehension

You probably know the language of fairy tales quite well. They often have well-known phrases, like the following:

- Once upon a time...
- They all lived happily ever after.

Fairy tales are for children and the language used reflects this, often using repetitive language.

Top tip

Read other fairy stories and look for common phrases used in them.

Comprehension material

Cinderella

Once upon a time, a grand invitation went out explaining that the Prince was holding a ball for all the young ladies in the land so that he could choose one to marry. The Ugly Sisters were very excited and bought new dresses for the occasion. They made Cinderella help them get ready for days in advance.

On the evening of the ball, the Ugly Sisters left and Cinderella sat down on the kitchen step and cried; she had nothing to wear and no way of getting to the ball. Suddenly, there was a swirl of colours and an old lady was standing in front of Cinderella.

"You shall go to the ball, Cinderella!" she said.

With that, the Fairy Godmother turned a pumpkin into a golden coach, then turned her wand on Cinderella. Suddenly, Cinderella was wearing an amazing ball gown, sparkling tiara and beautiful glass slippers. She would go to the ball!

"Have fun, but leave before midnight, as that is when the magic will wear off and you'll be back in your old clothes!" the Fairy Godmother said.

When Cinderella arrived at the ball she was a dazzling beauty whom nobody recognised. The Prince hurried to dance with her; the Ugly Sisters were furious! Cinderella was enjoying herself so much that she forgot the Fairy Godmother's warning. The clock began to strike midnight. She turned from the Prince, and ran down the stairs to her coach, accidently dropping one of her glass slippers on the way.

The next day the Prince and his servants went from house to house looking for the girl whose foot would fit the slipper. When they arrived at Cinderella's house, the Ugly Sisters were still in a towering rage. They tried the slipper on first; it didn't fit. Cinderella asked to try it; the sisters laughed, but the shoe fitted her perfectly. The Prince looked into Cinderella's face and saw the beautiful eyes from the night before. He married her the very next day and they lived happily ever after.

Practice activities

1. Write down the traditional opening and ending that are used in this story.

Opening: Once upon a time

Ending: they lived happily ever after

2. Who is the magical character in this story? How does the author describe this character?

fairy Godmother old lady

Test-style questions

1. Who was the "dazzling beauty"? Circle **one** answer.

Ugly Sister **Fairy Godmother** **Cinderella** **Prince** *1 mark*

2. Why were the Ugly Sisters "in a towering rage" the morning after the ball?

the glass slippers fit cinderella

2 marks

3. Put the following events in order, numbering them 1–5. The first one has been done for you.

Cinderella arrived at the ball.	3
The Fairy Godmother transformed Cinderella.	2
Cinderella helped the Ugly Sisters get ready for the ball.	1
Cinderella and the Prince got married.	5
The clock struck midnight.	4

2 marks

Themes in fairy tales

Key to comprehension

Fairy tales often involve princes and princesses who want to get married. Usually, as they are the good characters, their wishes come true and they are happily married by the end of the story! This is just one of a number of common **themes** that run through fairy tales. Others that you need to look out for include:

- good conquering evil
- characters seeking happiness
- heroic rescues.

Top tip

Read other fairy tales and look for common themes.

Comprehension material

The Princess and the Pea

Once upon a time there lived a prince who was very fed up. He wanted to get married. Everyone thought he should get married. The problem was that he would only marry a true princess. He had met many girls who *claimed* to be princesses, but they turned out not to be *true* princesses. The prince had given up hope and instead sat in the palace feeling miserable.

One night there was a terrible storm. Rain lashed down, thunder rumbled close by and lightning forks lit the sky around the palace. Everyone huddled together, close to the fire. Suddenly, the front door bell rang, cutting through the storm. The prince rushed to open the door.

Standing on the doorstep, dripping wet, was a princess…well, she said she was a princess but the prince would not be fooled so easily. She didn't look much like a princess in her dripping clothes and she was all alone, without a maid.

The queen decided to test the girl, so she instructed the maids to make up a bed in the second-best bedroom (not the best bedroom, as she might not be a princess). She told the maids to take all the bedding and the mattress from the bed and then placed one single pea in the middle of the bedframe. The maids then piled twenty-five mattresses and twenty-five soft quilts on top.

The girl was then left to sleep on the bed for the night. In the morning, the queen entered the bedroom and asked the girl how she had slept.

"I didn't sleep a wink all night long," replied the girl. "There was a great, hard lump in the middle of the bed – it was quite horrible."

Everyone knew by this that the girl was a true princess. The prince was so happy that he married her the very next day and they lived happily ever after.

Practice activities

1. Write down three characters that are in this story that are often found in other fairy tales.

2. How is the ending, and what happens to the characters, similar to other fairy tales?

Test-style questions

1. Why was the prince miserable at the start?

Tick **one**

He was fed up of eating peas. ☐

He couldn't find a real princess. ☐

He hated princesses. ☐

1 mark

2. In your own words, explain how everyone knew that the princess was "a true princess" by the end of the story.

2 marks

3. Why did the prince think that she was not a princess when he first saw her?

1 mark

The structure of myths

Key to comprehension

Myths are stories about gods and goddesses. Many have a religious message. Some have a message about what happens because of people's wishes or actions.

Many myths are about amazing events and characters, animals and objects that have magical powers.

Top tip

Read other myths and look for common themes and characters.

Comprehension material

The Midas Touch

Midas was king of Phrygia. One day his farmhands brought him a creature who was part-man and part-goat. They had found him sleeping in the vineyard and tied him up to stop him escaping. Midas immediately recognised the creature as Silenus, who was the right-hand man to the god Dionysus. He quickly ordered that he be set free.

Silenus explained that he and his master had just returned from the East where they had been discussing the cultivation of the grape. Dionysus had brought back a tiger or two and an ever-expanding flock of followers, as well as a very tired Silenus. Silenus had slept in Midas's vineyard to recover from the trip. Now he (and Dionysus) were grateful to the king for treating him well. The god was so pleased, in fact, that he offered to grant whatever Midas should wish for.

Midas didn't have to think twice; he believed that he would be happy if he could continually restock the gold in his royal treasury, so he asked that everything he touch be turned to gold. Dionysus paused, checked twice whether this is what Midas really wanted, and then waved his sceptre and the wish was granted.

Midas quickly returned home to have a go. He was unsure to begin with and laid a shaking hand on a bowl of fruit and then a stool. Each of these turned to the purest gold.

"Look at this!" he boasted, turning his chariot into solid gold (which made it worthless as it could no longer move). He then took his young daughter by the hand to show her more, forgetting that she would turn to gold – a golden statue.

"Oh no!" cried Midas. As he touched more things he realised that he couldn't touch any useful object without it becoming useless (yet priceless) , nor any food, nor any person.

It was at this point that Midas understood why Dionysus had been reluctant to grant the wish and had checked with him twice before granting it.

Fortunately, Dionysus was very kind, and very forgiving. He allowed Midas to wash away his magic touch in the river Pactolus.

Practice activities

1. What is the name of the god who is in this story?

____

2. In your own words, what did Midas learn in this myth?

____

____

____

Test-style questions

1. Who was the creature sleeping in the vineyard?

Circle **one** answer.

a goat **Silenus** **Dionysus** **Midas** *1 mark*

2. How many times did Dionysus check with Midas about his wish?

Circle **one** answer.

once **three times** **five times** **twice** *1 mark*

3. Why was Midas unsure to start with when he had his wish?

____

____

2 marks

4. Why do you think Dionysus let Midas reverse his wish?

____

____

2 marks

Themes of legends

Key to comprehension

Legends, like myths, tell us about how people lived, what they believed, what they valued and what they were afraid of. Legends have many of the **themes** that are used in traditional stories. For example:

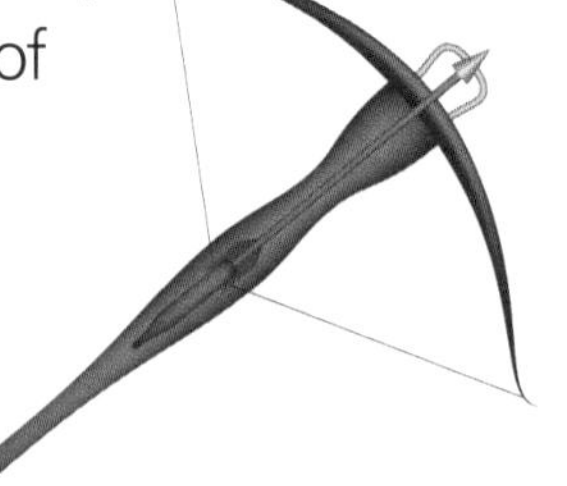

- good vs evil / wise vs foolish / strong vs weak / just vs unjust
- magic and the supernatural
- rags to riches / riches to rags
- a quest, a search or a journey.

Comprehension material

William Tell

One day, William Tell decided to go to his nearest town with his son, Walter, to collect provisions. When they reached the town they immediately felt uneasy as there were soldiers everywhere. As they walked across the square, Tell noticed a tall pole with an expensive hat perched on top and soldiers guarding it. He thought it very strange to have a hat on a pole! He pulled his son closer and carried on walking.

Suddenly, guards surrounded them saying they had not obeyed the new rule, which was to bow to the hat on the pole to show that the Austrian governor, Gessler, was more important than the Swiss people. Tell knew it would be safer to obey, but he was angry that the Swiss people were being humiliated in this way. He told the guards that he would not do as they had asked.

He was immediately arrested and the guards went to fetch the governor, Gessler. When Gessler arrived, he demanded to know why Tell would not bow to the hat. Tell told him he did not want to. Gessler said he was a stupid Swiss man and told the guards to imprison him. Just as Gessler was leaving, Walter called after him and said that his father was not stupid; in fact, he was the best shot with a crossbow in the whole of Switzerland.

Gessler said he would let Tell go if he could hit an apple on the head of Walter at a hundred paces. Tell refused to put his son in danger, but Gessler said that he would kill Walter if he did not accept the challenge. William Tell had no choice.

Tell was nervous, but Walter reassured him. Walter trusted his father completely and showed him he was not afraid. Tell took two bolts from his quiver and fired one. *Thwack!* The apple splintered into hundreds of pieces. The Swiss people cheered. Tell made to leave with his son.

Gessler stopped him to ask what the second bolt was for. Tell told him that, had it gone wrong, he would have used it to shoot him. When Gessler told the guards to arrest Tell and his son, Tell had no choice but to use the bolt to rid the world of Gessler, thus giving the Swiss people their freedom once again.

Practice activities

1. Using the themes in the *Key to comprehension* section, which two themes do you think this story reflects?

____________________ and ____________________

2. Do you think it was right of William Tell to kill the governor? Explain your answer.

____

____

Test-style questions

1. What was the name of the governor? Circle **one** answer.

William Tell **Walter Tell** **Gessler** **Emperor** *1 mark*

2. When Walter and William first arrived in the town, what made them uneasy?

____

1 mark

3. Would you have bowed to the hat?

YES **NO** (circle **one**)

Explain your answer.

____

____

1 mark

4. Write the sentence that shows that Tell hit the apple from Walter's head.

____

1 mark

Complex characters

Key to comprehension

Some **characters** are good role models, showing us how we should behave. For example:

- Superman
- Little Red Riding Hood.

Some characters show us how not to behave. For example:

- The Big Bad Wolf
- Voldermort.

However, like people in real life, characters can be bad in one moment but good in the next. Like us, they don't always understand why they do things and can be quite **complex**.

Comprehension material

Extract from *The Lion, the Witch and the Wardrobe* by C. S. Lewis

You mustn't think that even now Edmund was quite so bad that he actually wanted his brother and sisters to be turned into stone. He did want Turkish Delight and to be a Prince (and later a King) and to pay Peter out for calling him a beast. As for what the Witch would do with the others, he didn't want her to be particularly nice to them – certainly not to put them on the same level as himself; but he managed to believe, or to pretend he believed, that she wouldn't do anything very bad to them, "Because," he said to himself, "all these people who say nasty things about her are her enemies and probably half of it isn't true. She was jolly nice to me, anyway, much nicer than they are. I expect she is the rightful Queen really. Anyway, she'll be better than that awful Aslan!" At least, that was the excuse he made in his own mind for what he was doing. It wasn't a very good excuse, however, for deep down inside him he really knew that the White Witch was bad and cruel.

Practice activities

1. Name **two** things that Edmund wants that the White Witch could give him.

____________________ and ____________________

2. Do you think Edmund, from this extract, is a good or bad character? Why?

____

____

____

Test-style questions

1. What is the name of Edmund's brother? Circle **one** answer.

   Peter **White Witch** **Edmund** **Aslan** *1 mark*

2. Did Edmund want his brother and sisters turned to stone?

   YES **NO** (circle **one**)

   Explain your answer.

   ____

   ____

   2 marks

3. Did Edmund truly believe the excuse that he made up?

   YES **NO** (circle **one**)

   Explain how you know.

   ____

   ____

   ____

   2 marks

Key to comprehension

It is the author's job to let us know the personality of the character and this is called **characterisation**.

Characters need to be life-like and this is achieved by describing their behaviour and the decisions they make, what they say and how they say it.

At times, an author may choose to reveal the thoughts that run through a character's mind.

Comprehension material

Extract from *The Railway Children* by Edith Nesbit

The Station Master loosened Peter's collar, struck a match and looked at them by its flickering light.

"Why," said he, "you're the children from the Three Chimneys up yonder. So nicely dressed, too. Tell me now, what made you do such a thing? Haven't you been to church? …" He spoke much more gently now, and Peter said:–

"I didn't think it was stealing. I was almost sure it wasn't. I thought if I took it from the outside part of the heap, perhaps it would be. But in the middle I thought I could fairly count it only mining. It'll take thousands of years for you to burn up all that coal and get to the middle parts."

"Not quite. But did you do it for a lark* or what?"

"Not much lark carting that beastly heavy stuff up the hill," said Peter, indignantly.

"Then why did you?" The Station Master's voice was so much kinder now that Peter replied:–

"You know that wet day? Well, Mother said we were too poor to have a fire. We always had fires when it was cold at our other house, and –"

"DON'T!" interrupted Bobbie, in a whisper.

"Well," said the Station Master, rubbing his chin thoughtfully, "I'll tell you what I'll do. I'll look over it this once…"

**A lark is a harmless joke or a bit of fun.*

Practice activities

1. Why did Peter take the coal?

___

___

2. Why do you think the Station Master let Peter off this time?

___

Test-style questions

1. What did Peter think he was doing in the middle of the coal pile? Circle **one** answer.

   stealing **borrowing** **mining** **digging** *1 mark*

2. Do you think Peter is a bad character?

   YES **NO** (circle **one**)

   Explain your answer, using evidence from the text.

   ___

   ___

   1 mark

3. Do you think that what Peter did was stealing?

   YES **NO** (circle **one**)

   Explain your answer.

   ___

   ___

   ___

   2 marks

Drawing inferences 1

Key to comprehension

An **inference** is a conclusion or a judgement based on evidence or reasoning.

In books, authors often *tell* you more than they *say* directly. They give clues or hints that help the reader "read between the lines".

When you use these clues to give you a better understanding of the text, it is called **inferring**.

Top tip

When reading, look at all of the information to help you infer deeper meaning in a text.

Comprehension material

Extract from *Grimble* by Clement Freud

One Monday Grimble came back from school, opened the door and shouted, "I am home." No one shouted anything in answer. So he went round the house looking for messages because his parents always left messages. It was the one thing they were really good at.

On a table in the sitting room there was a globe. And stuck into the globe were two pins, each with a triangle of paper on it. One of these was stuck into England and said *Grimble*, and the other was stuck into Peru and said *us*. He went into the kitchen and here was another note: *Tea is in the fridge, sandwiches in the oven. Have a good time.*

In the bedroom was a note saying *You will do your homework, won't you? P.S. don't forget to say your prayers.*

In the bathroom a message *Teeth.*

He walked round the house thinking they've really been very good, and then he went to the back-door and saw a note: *Milkman. No milk for five days.*

He changed the note to *Not much milk* for five days, and sat down in the kitchen and started to think about things. Five days is a long time for anyone and an especially long time for a boy of ten who is never quite sure whether he might not be missing his birthday. It had been weeks since he last had a birthday. He got a piece of paper and worked out five days at twenty-four hours a day and made it over a hundred hours, actually a hundred and something hours. He decided to have a sandwich. He opened the oven door, found the oven absolutely full of sandwiches, and took one with corned beef and apricot jam in it.

Practice activities

1. Do you think Grimble's parents are being good parents? Circle **Yes** or **No**.

   Explain your answer.

   ____

   ____

2. What do you think the message *"Teeth"* meant?

   ____

Test-style questions

1. What was the one thing that Grimble's parents were really good at?

   Tick **one**

   reading him bedtime stories ☐

   being good parents ☐

   making sandwiches ☐

   leaving messages ☐

   1 mark

2. Why did the note that his parents had written for the milkman make Grimble think that they had not been so good after all?

   ____

   ____

   1 mark

3. How long are Grimble's parents planning to be away? How do you know?

   ____

   ____

   2 marks

Key to comprehension

Here is an example of how authors tell you more than they say directly:

Freya looked at her watch, grabbed her bag and ran to the school bus stop. When she got there, she realised that she had forgotten her lunchbox. Instead of going back for it, she got on the bus.

We know that Freya catches the bus to school, can read the time on a watch, took her bag with her and forgot her lunch because the author says so directly. We can **infer** that she is running late, that she only just got to the bus stop on time (as she could not go back for her lunch), and that she will need to find lunch at school or go without.

Comprehension material

The Lion and the Mouse

A lion, who was king of the jungle, was bored and fed up. He watched a mouse collecting food for its family before he trapped its tail under his enormous paw.

"Please don't eat me!" squeaked the mouse. "My family needs this food. I promise to help you one day when you are most in need."

The lion laughed. "How will you ever be able to help me? But, you are a brave little mouse so I will let you go."

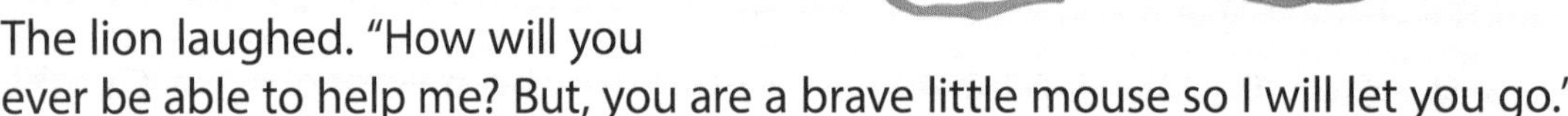

A few days later, hunters managed to catch the lion in a big, strong net. The lion was angry and roared so that the whole jungle could hear him. He wriggled about, trying to free himself but only managed to get himself more tangled. Despite his strength, he could not break the net.

Suddenly, the little mouse appeared. Without hesitation, he chewed through the net and the lion was soon free.

"Thank you, my friend," said the lion. "I did not believe you when you said that you would be able to help me one day, but now I do! I freed you and now you have set me free!"

Practice activities

1. Write down **two** things that the author has *told* you.
   e.g. The lion was bored and fed up at the start of the story.

   a) ______________________________

   b) ______________________________

2. Write down **two** things that you can *infer* about the characters.
   e.g. The mouse's family are waiting at home for their food.

   a) ______________________________

   b) ______________________________

Test-style questions

1. How did the lion set the mouse free?

   Tick **one**

   He stopped the monkeys from hurting him. ☐

   He helped the mouse to chew through the net. ☐

   He let him go instead of eating him. ☐

   1 mark

2. Why did the lion laugh and question how the mouse could ever help him?

   ____

   ____

   2 marks

3. What did the lion learn about the mouse in the story?

   ____

   ____

   1 mark

Justifying inferences 1

Key to comprehension

Sometimes you will be asked to **justify** your inferences. In order to do this, you will need to use evidence from the text (e.g. what the author actually says) to explain how you came to your conclusion.

Comprehension material

Shipwreck

It was early morning when we heard the church bells ringing. It wasn't Sunday so we knew there wasn't a church service. There was only one thing it could be. A shipwreck!

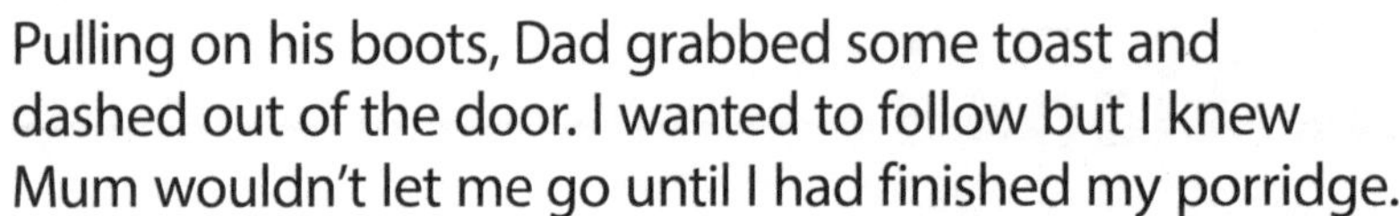

Pulling on his boots, Dad grabbed some toast and dashed out of the door. I wanted to follow but I knew Mum wouldn't let me go until I had finished my porridge.

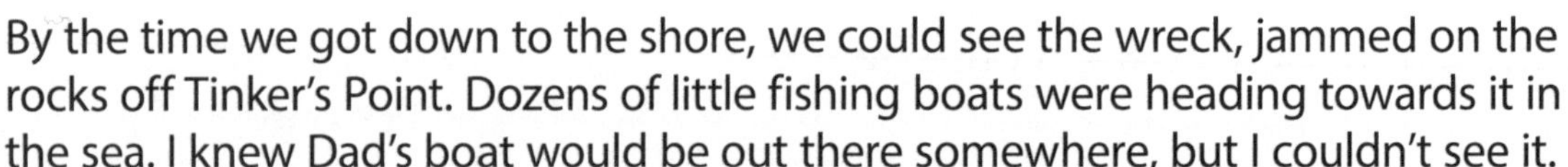

By the time we got down to the shore, we could see the wreck, jammed on the rocks off Tinker's Point. Dozens of little fishing boats were heading towards it in the sea. I knew Dad's boat would be out there somewhere, but I couldn't see it.

Boats were wrecked on those rocks every year. I knew the ship would not sink for now. It would be stuck on the rocks until the tide washed it free later in the day. There was always plenty of time to rescue the crew.

The barrels and crates the ship was carrying were another matter. Once the men from the ship were safely ashore, anyone with a little boat would be back in the water again, fishing for crates of colourful silk, fancy tea sets or spices from far away.

Practice activities

1. From this text you could make the following inference: **the narrator has seen ships wrecked on those rocks before**.

   Write down two pieces of evidence to justify this inference.

   a) ______________________________

   b) ______________________________

2. The little fishing boats were going out to rescue the crew first.

How do you know this?

____

____

Test-style questions

1. How do the villagers know that there has been a shipwreck?

Tick **two**

The rocks are dangerous. ☐

The church bells are ringing. ☐

Somebody is shouting it. ☐

It is not Sunday. ☐

1 mark

2. What did the narrator have to finish before leaving the house? Circle **one** answer.

breakfast **lunch** **dinner** **a snack**

1 mark

3. Why do you think that the narrator "knew Dad's boat would be out there somewhere"?

____

____

2 marks

4. How does the narrator know that the crew will be saved?

____

____

2 marks

Justifying inferences 2

Key to comprehension

Justifying inferences is an important skill. You need to first draw a conclusion or make a judgement about something that you are told by an author. You must then scan the text further, to identify evidence that supports your inference. If you can't find any, you might need to rethink your inference.

Top tip

As you read, look for clues in the text that give you extra information about characters or events.

Comprehension material

Extract from *The Wonderful Wizard of Oz* by L. Frank Baum

Just as he spoke there came from the forest a terrible roar, and the next moment a great Lion bounded into the road. With one blow of his paw he sent the Scarecrow spinning over and over to the edge of the road, and then he struck at the Tin Woodman with his sharp claws. But, to the Lion's surprise, he could make no impression on the tin, although the Woodman fell over in the road and lay still.

Little Toto, now that he had an enemy to face, ran barking toward the Lion, and the great beast had opened his mouth to bite the dog, when Dorothy, fearing Toto would be killed, and heedless of danger, rushed forward and slapped the Lion upon his nose as hard as she could, while she cried out:

"Don't you dare to bite Toto! You ought to be ashamed of yourself, a big beast like you, to bite a poor little dog!"

"I didn't bite him," said the Lion, as he rubbed his nose with his paw where Dorothy had hit it.

"No, but you tried to," she retorted. "You are nothing but a big coward."

"I know it," said the Lion, hanging his head in shame. "I've always known it. But how can I help it?"

"I don't know, I'm sure. To think of your striking a stuffed man, like the poor Scarecrow!"

Practice activities

1. Why does Dorothy think (**infer**) that the Lion is a "big coward"?

2. Why did the Scarecrow fall over so easily?

Test-style questions

1. What did they hear before they saw the lion? Circle **one** answer.

a horrible roar **a terrible roar** **a terrifying roar** **a loud roar**

1 mark

2. Who slapped the lion on the nose? Circle **one** answer.

Tin Woodman **Scarecrow** **Toto** **Dorothy** *1 mark*

3. How many characters in this extract are actually struck by the Lion?

1 mark

4. What is a coward?

1 mark

5. Write down the phrase that Dorothy uses to describe Toto.

1 mark

Key to comprehension

Play scripts are written versions of a play that are used by the actors in preparation for a performance. The actors use the script during rehearsals so that they can practise the play. They need to think about how the characters are feeling and then say the lines with the right kind of emotion. By the final performance they must know the script by heart.

Top tip

The writing in italics (stage directions) is not read aloud. It gives details about how to speak or act, or what the scenery looks like.

Comprehension material

Who's missing?

The scene is a classroom with the children sitting in groups around tables and the teacher standing at the front at her computer.

TEACHER Shh! I am going to do the register now and I need to know who is missing as there are some empty spaces. Please do not speak whilst I do the register. Jamie…

Silence.

TEACHER That's a good start. Jamie isn't here. I felt sure I had seen him this morning. Oh well, Megan…

Silence.

TEACHER And Megan is away as well…This is not a good day. I hope they are not poorly. Mark…

Silence.

TEACHER Oh dear, I hope that some people are here *(laughing and looking up from the register)*. Phoebe…

Georgia has her hand in the air and is making noises to attract Teacher.

TEACHER What is it, Georgia? I told you not to interrupt during the register.

GEORGIA Mrs Thomas, you didn't say don't interrupt. You said not to *speak* while you did the register…so nobody has.

TEACHER *(sigh)* What is your point Georgia? Hurry up…

GEORGIA Well, Jamie, Megan, Mark and Phoebe are all here but you told them not to speak so they didn't answer their names.

TEACHER *(big sigh)* Oh dear, it is not going well this morning. Please, just tell me who is missing!

Practice activities

1. Work with a partner. Each read the words of a character in the play. Use the script to help you to act the play.

   Use the stage directions (the parts in italics) to help you make it realistic.

2. Circle the word that best describes how the teacher is feeling. You may need to use a dictionary.

   bored **amused** **furious** **exasperated**

Test-style questions

1. What is the name of the teacher? Circle **one** answer.

   Mr James **Miss Thomas** **Thomas** **Mrs Thomas** *1 mark*

2. Why did the children not answer when the teacher read out their names?

   ____

   ____

   1 mark

3. What instruction did the teacher mean to give to the children at the start of the register?

   ____

   ____

   1 mark

4. If the register is in alphabetical order by **surname**, draw lines to link the first and second names of the children, based on the order they were read out.

   One has been done for you.

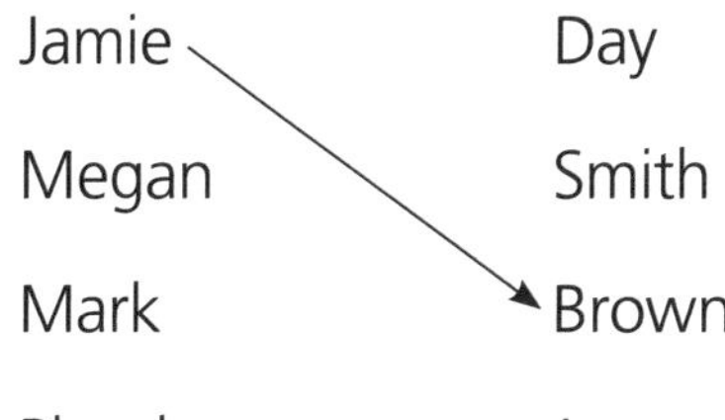

1 mark

The structure of play scripts

Key to comprehension

A play script shows the lines that need to be said next to each character's name. It also shows **stage directions**, which give the actors information about how they should say their lines, how they should move and position themselves, where the scene is set, what scenery there is, and how any **props** (moveable stage items) should be used.

Top tip

Learn the key features of play scripts and you will be able to read and understand any play script!

Comprehension material

Who is the best?

The scene is a jungle clearing with a rock that Tiger is standing on at the beginning of the play. All the other animals are gathered around him.

TIGER: *(proudly)* I am the fiercest animal in this jungle and therefore I must be the best!

MONKEY: *(a little bit scared)* Mr Tiger, are there not other things that are important?

TIGER: *(laughing)* What could be more important than being fierce?

EAGLE: *(flying up to the rock next to Tiger)* What about being able to fly above the jungle and look for danger to warn others?

TIGER: Pah! I don't need warning. I am the fiercest and the best!

Eagle flies off.

ELEPHANT: What about being the tallest and biggest animal in the jungle?

TIGER: What use is that if you are not fiercer than me?

Elephant walks off shaking his head.

CROCODILE: What about having the biggest set of teeth and being able to hide in the water?

TIGER: Um… your teeth are impressive, but you are still not as fierce as me.

Crocodile slithers off into the water.

MONKEY: *(still a little scared)* What about Mr Monkey being able to make a loud noise and swing through the trees?

TIGER: What is the use of that, you silly monkey? Like I said, fiercest is the best!

Monkey swings off through the trees.

SNAKE: *(slithering along the ground)* What about being camouflaged so you can creep up on your prey? *(opens mouth and goes to attack the Tiger with a hissing sound).*

TIGER: OK, OK! There are better things than being fierce. Please don't hurt me!

Practice activities

1. How many characters have speaking parts in this scene? ______________

2. What are the stage directions for in this scene?

____

____

Test-style questions

1. Who thinks being able to hide in the water is better than being the fiercest? Circle **one** answer.

   Monkey **Crocodile** **Eagle** **Snake**

   1 mark

2. Why does Tiger change his mind about the fiercest being the best?

   ____

   ____

   1 mark

3. Do you think that any animal in the play is better than the others?

   YES **NO** (circle **one**)

   Explain your answer.

   ____

   ____

   ____

   ____

   2 marks

The language of poetry

Key to comprehension

Poems can be about almost anything. Poems can be very intense and sometimes they do not use very many words.

It is important to understand that whilst some poems **rhyme**, not all poems have to rhyme.

Rhythm is often very important in poetry.

Sometimes sentences can be broken up into separate lines on the page, and sometimes the lines can be grouped together in **stanzas**. Stanzas are normally separated by a line space.

Comprehension material

On with the Show

Falling silently from leaden skies
with dancing, drifting clusters
of spiny webs,
winter takes a bow.

Beneath the crystal covering,
spring waits in the wings.
Chorus lines of snowdrops waiting
and it's on with the show.

Practice activities

1. How many stanzas does this poem have? ______________

Pages 4–5
Practice activities

1. It was written some time ago and is still read today.
2. telegram

Test-style questions

1. 7 *(**1 mark**)*
2. summer *(**1 mark**)*
3. He was pretending to be a sailboat tacking against the wind. *(**2 marks** for answering that he was being a sailboat tacking against the wind; **1 mark** for an answer that states that he was a boat but does not mention the wind.)*
4. lake, Holly Howe *(**1 mark** for each correct answer on the correct line.)*
5. "just engines in tin boxes" *(**1 mark** for direct quote from the text.)*

Pages 6–7
Practice activities

1. Badger, Mole, Rat and Toad
2. ferrets and weasels

Test-style questions

1. Rat *(**1 mark**)*
2. a stick / cudgel *(**1 mark**)*
3. in a hall *(**1 mark**)*
4. dive *(**1 mark**)*

Pages 8–9
Practice activities

1. quietly / gently
2. the wind outside

Test-style questions

1. a fairy *(**1 mark**)*
2. fairy language *(**1 mark**)*
3. That he has come through the window and landed on the floor as if from nowhere (as if he has been dropped from the sky). *(**2 marks** for answering he has come through the window **and** a link to appearing from nowhere; **1 mark** for an answer that identifies he has come through the window but does not link to the word "dropped".)*
4. "the big box" *(**1 mark** for this direct quote from the text.)*

Pages 10–11
Practice activities

1. *Any of the following:* the fairy; the talking frog; the bewitching of the prince; the frog turning into a prince.
2. She was rude, ungrateful and unkind to people.

Test-style questions

1. her parents *(**1 mark**)*
2. She was shocked / surprised to find that the frog was able to talk. *(**1 mark** for an answer that states that the frog could talk.)*
3. She was hungry but she did not want to eat from the same plate as the frog because she was cross / unhappy / thought it was unhygienic. *(**2 marks** for answering that she was hungry but did not want to share the plate with the frog; **1 mark** for an answer that identifies she didn't want to share the plate with the frog but does not link this with her being hungry.)*
4. He learned that it was better to be kind, polite and helpful rather than rude and demanding. *(**1 mark** for an answer that identifies that he learned that he should treat people well.)*

Pages 12–13
Practice activities

1. **Opening:** Once upon a time;
   Ending: lived happily ever after.
2. an old lady; Fairy Godmother

Test-style questions

1. Cinderella *(**1 mark**)*
2. They were angry because the Prince had only danced with the mystery girl and they had wanted to dance with him and eventually marry him. *(**2 marks** for answering that they were angry with the mystery girl for dancing with the Prince **and** that they had wanted to dance with

*him / marry him; **1 mark** for an answer that identifies one of the above but does not link them.)*

3. Cinderella arrived at the ball. 3
   The Fairy Godmother transformed Cinderella. 2
   Cinderella helped the Ugly Sisters get ready for the ball. 1
   Cinderella and the Prince got married. 5
   The clock struck midnight. 4
   *(**2 marks** for all in correct order.)*

Pages 14–15

Practice activities

1. prince; princess; queen (maid also possible)
2. Fairy tales usually end with the good characters living happily ever after / getting married, like they do in this one.

Test-style questions

1. He couldn't find a real princess. *(**1 mark**)*
2. Because the princess could feel the pea under twenty-five mattresses and twenty-five quilts, which was a test and something only a princess would be sensitive enough to feel. *(**2 marks** for linking the feeling of the pea to this being a test for being a princess; **1 mark** for stating that she felt the pea.)*
3. *Any one of the following:* She did not have a maid / She was on her own / Her clothes were dripping *(**1 mark**)*.

Pages 16–17

Practice activities

1. Dionysus
2. Midas learned not to be greedy and that although things can be worth a lot of money when they are gold, some things are better as they are.

Test-style questions

1. Silenus *(**1 mark**)*
2. twice *(**1 mark**)*
3. He had been given a new skill and he didn't know if it would work. *(**2 marks** for linking the new skill with the not knowing if it would work; **1 mark** for stating that it was a new skill **or** he didn't know if it would work.)*
4. Dionysus knew that Midas had learned his lesson and that he would not be greedy again *(**1 mark**)*. He also knew that he could not carry on living in that way *(**1 mark**)*.

Pages 18–19

Practice activities

1. *Any two from the following:* good vs evil; just vs unjust; strong vs weak; wise vs foolish
2. **Yes**, I think it was right because the governor had gone back on his promise to let William Tell's son go and he was mean to the local people. He would probably have killed William Tell anyway.
   Or...
   No, I think he should not have killed the governor because you should never kill people. You should find another way to sort things out.

Test-style questions

1. Gessler *(**1 mark**)*
2. the number of soldiers *(**1 mark**)*
3. **Yes**, because it would have meant that I was safe.
   Or...
   No, because Gessler was a bully.
   *(**1 mark** for circling an answer and writing a plausible explanation that matches the circled answer.)*
4. "The apple splintered into hundreds of pieces." *(**1 mark**)*

Pages 20–21

Practice activities

1. *Any two of the following:* Turkish Delight; to be a Prince; to be a King; to pay Peter back for being mean
2. **Good**, because he did not really want

his brother and sisters harmed.

Or...

Bad, because he wants to betray his brother and sisters and find the White Witch, even though he knows she is bad. *(Either answer would be acceptable as long as it is backed up with evidence from the text.)*

Test-style questions

1. Peter *(**1 mark**)*
2. **No**, because it says that he didn't in the text. *(**1 mark** for circling **No**; **1 mark** for an explanation that states that the answer is in the text.)*
3. **No**, because at the end it says that deep down he knew that the Witch was cruel. *(**1 mark** for circling **No**; **1 mark** for an explanation that uses evidence from the text.)*

Pages 22–23

Practice activities

1. Because he wanted to be able to provide coal for the family, even though they were poor.
2. He felt sorry for them when Peter explained why he had done it.

Test-style questions

1. mining *(**1 mark**)*
2. **No**, because he took the coal to look after his family.

   Or...

   Yes, because it is wrong to steal.
   *(**1 mark** for circling an answer and writing a plausible explanation that matches the circled answer.)*
3. **Yes** *(**1 mark**)*, because he took something that did not belong to him without permission *(**1 mark**)*.

Pages 24–25

Practice activities

1. **No**, because they have left him at home all by himself and gone to a different country without telling him.
2. It is in the bathroom, so they want him to remember to clean his teeth.

Test-style questions

1. leaving messages *(**1 mark**)*
2. Because they had cancelled the milk which meant he wouldn't have any while they were gone. *(**1 mark**)*
3. 5 days *(**1 mark**)* because they have asked the milkman not to leave any milk for 5 days *(**1 mark**)*.

Pages 26–27

Practice activities

1. *Any two things that are written down in the story:* e.g. the lion caught the mouse in his paw; the mouse told the lion he would help him one day.
2. *Any of the following or any other plausible inference from the text:* the lion wasn't hungry because he did not eat the mouse immediately; the lion thought the mouse was too small to ever be able to help him; the hunters took the lion by surprise as he could have eaten them otherwise; the mouse heard the lion roar and came to help him.

Test-style questions

1. He let him go instead of eating him. *(**1 mark**)*
2. The lion laughed because the mouse was so small *(**1 mark**)*. He is so big and did not believe that he would ever need help from a mouse *(**1 mark**)*.
3. That even though he was small, he could be helpful to the lion. *(**1 mark**)*

Pages 28–29

Practice activities

1. The narrator knows what the ringing bells mean / "boats were wrecked on those rocks every year" / the narrator knows that the ship won't sink "for now" / using the word "always" when talking about rescuing the crew shows it has happened before / knowing that the

boats will go out again after the crew are rescued *(any two of these would be acceptable).*

2. The final paragraph says once the men from the ship were safely ashore, the boats would go back out again.

Test-style questions

1. The church bells are ringing; It is not Sunday. *(**1 mark** for ticking both correct answers.)*
2. breakfast *(**1 mark**)*
3. His dad had put his boots on and rushed out of the house *(**1 mark**)*, and he must own a boat for the narrator to say "Dad's boat" *(**1 mark**)*.
4. The text says "I knew the ship would not sink for now" *(**1 mark**)* and "There was always plenty of time to rescue the crew" *(**1 mark**)*.

Pages 30–31

Practice activities

1. He is big and strong and he is trying to hurt helpless people and a little dog.
2. He is stuffed with straw and therefore light, not like a human.

Test-style questions

1. a terrible roar *(**1 mark**)*
2. Dorothy *(**1 mark**)*
3. 2 *(**1 mark**)*
4. A person who lacks the courage to do the right thing or endure dangerous or unpleasant things. *(**1 mark** for a correct explanation – this may be from a dictionary.)*
5. "a poor little dog". *(**1 mark** for this direct quotation.)*

Pages 32–33

Practice activities

1. Check that the child is only saying the parts for their character, and not reading the stage directions aloud.
2. exasperated

Test-style questions

1. Mrs Thomas *(**1 mark**)*
2. She had told them not to speak whilst she did the register. *(**1 mark**)*
3. Not to speak unless they were answering their names. *(**1 mark**)*
4. Megan Day, Mark Jones, Phoebe Smith *(**1 mark**)*

Pages 34–35

Practice activities

1. six
2. To give the actors information about how they should say their lines / move / position themselves / what scenery there is.

Test-style questions

1. Crocodile *(**1 mark**)*
2. The snake is about to attack him. *(**1 mark**)*
3. **No** *(**1 mark**)*, because each animal has different strengths and weaknesses and therefore you cannot compare them with each other *(**1 mark**)*.

Pages 36–37

Practice activities

1. two
2. It rhymes.

Test-style questions

1. winter *(**1 mark**)*
2. the wings at the edge of a stage *(**1 mark**)*
3. snowdrops *(**1 mark**)*
4. **Winter** is turning into **spring**. *(**1 mark** for the seasons written in the correct order.)*
5. The snow / ice / frost that is covering the surface of the ground *(**1 mark**)*.

Pages 38–39

Practice activities

1. At the end of the fifth and sixth lines the poet has used **rhyming**. Within these lines she has used **repetition**.
2. weird, woman, woods

Test-style questions

1. bugs *(**1 mark**)*
2. thinner *(**1 mark**)*
3. creaky and squeaky *(**1 mark**)*
4. Individual answers based on child's own opinions. *(**2 marks** for an answer that gives a plausible reason for either **Yes** or **No**, and that refers to the actual text; **1 mark** for a reason that is based purely on personal preference, without reference to the actual text.)*

Pages 40–41
Practice activities

1. The beginning – it is setting the scene for the story.
2. 500 years

Test-style questions

1. rats *(**1 mark**)*
2. made nests in them *(**1 mark**)*
3. By making lots of noise so they couldn't hear each other. *(**1 mark**)*
4. Hanover *(**1 mark**)*
5. cradles *(**1 mark**)*

Pages 42–43
Practice activities

1. An acrostic, because the first letters of each line spell SCHOOL.
2. A list poem, because it is a list of things that the child learned at school.

Test-style questions

1. to be able to stay in bed *(**1 mark**)*
2. second helpings *(**1 mark**)*
3. She does not want to hear about the naughty things the child has done. *(**1 mark**)*
4. *Examples:* They learned to read and write / to do something difficult in maths / to play a new game. *(**1 mark** for each plausible answer, up to a maximum of **2 marks**.)*

Pages 44–45
Practice activities

1. He doesn't think the manager cares about the environment.
2. illegal logging in Thailand / the threat to the habitats of people and birds / the destruction of the natural barrier against global warming

Test-style questions

1. The Furniture Store *(**1 mark**)*
2. Sam's *(**1 mark**)*
3. *Example answers:* Do you want to keep the table? / Where did you get your information from? / If you are worried about the environment, why did you buy the table? *(**1 mark** for a question that refers to Sam's complaint and action.)*

Pages 46–47
Practice activities

1. **Where:** penguin enclosure at the zoo
   When: 12.15pm on Saturday
   Why witness was there: waiting to watch penguins feed
2. *Example answer:* A girl dropped her camera into the penguin enclosure. Her dad was cross. He lifted her over the wall. She wanted to get nearer to the penguins. Her dad shouted because he thought they were attacking her. The keeper lifted her and the camera out. *(Check that the explanation is no more than 50 words long.)*

Test-style questions

1. her dad *(**1 mark**)*
2. No, because she wanted to get nearer to them, and she did not run away or cry when they approached her. *(**2 marks** for stating **No** with an explanation from the text; **1 mark** for stating **No** but with an explanation that is not based on the text.)*
3. **No** *(**1 mark**)*, the penguins were friendly and one of them nuzzled her hand *(**1 mark**)*.

Pages 48–49
Practice activities

1. Dorset

2. Deep Sea Adventure, Sharky's, Brewers Quay, Nothe Fort Museum of Coastal Defence, Sea Life Park

Test-style questions

1. Nothe Fort Museum *(**1 mark**)*
2. Christmas *(**1 mark**)*
3. amazing *(**1 mark**)*
4. *Example answer:* Nothe Fort Museum, because I would like to learn about maritime history. *(**1 mark** for each individual answer that is backed up with information given about the place in the guide.)*

Pages 50–51

Practice activities

1. Email, because of the address at the top of the page, the icons and the layout features.
2. *Example answers:* Hi / How are you doing? / use of contractions like 'isn't' / BTW / loads and loads of hugs

Test-style questions

1. Australia *(**1 mark**)*
2. Rebecca *(**1 mark**)*
3. **No**, because Freya asks her about her new house and school, which means she is living there, not just there on holiday. *(**2 marks** for circling **No** and giving reasons based on evidence from the text; **1 mark** for circling **No** but reason not based on textual evidence.)*
4. **Yes** – "which is keeping me busy and is annoying" *(**2 marks** for circling **Yes** and quoting the line from the text; **1 mark** for circling **Yes** but not using the quotation from the text.)*

Pages 52–53

Practice activities

1. The **author** has used **sub-headings** to help structure this **explanation** text and help the **reader** understand it in more detail.
2. The diagram shows the water cycle and how water rises and falls, which is what the paragraph is describing.

Test-style questions

1. water vapour *(**1 mark**)*
2. hydropower *(**1 mark**)*
3. Water *(**1 mark**)*, as the text says that electricity can be created by water *(**1 mark**)*.

Pages 54–55

Practice activities

1. Diary, because it says "Dear Diary" at the beginning.
2. wicked / mum / dad / granny / grandpa / best bit / Daddy / didn't / well / cool / thing / stuff / cos / fab / loads / I'm / gonna / gotta / tho / boo *(any three taken from the examples here.)*

Test-style questions

1. Grandpa *(**1 mark**)*
2. inflatable boat *(**1 mark**)*
3.

wins on 2p machines	Daddy
owns a 'cool bucket thing'	Granny
pulled boat in fast	Matilda

*(**2 marks** for all three correct; **1 mark** for one correct.)*

4. *Example answer:* My cousin had a bucket which made little sandcastles and which allowed you to stick arms, eyes, ears and other funny features on it (just like Mr Potato Head). I was quite jealous because it was great fun, but Matilda let me share it, so I got to play with it a lot too. *(**2 marks** for a paragraph that contains the same information in a formal tone; **1 mark** for a paragraph that has mostly formal, but some informal, words / tone.)*

Pages 56–57

Practice activities

1. *Any three of the following:* to retell an event or series of events; to tell someone how to make or do something; to discuss an issue or offer two or more points of

view; to give an account of how or why something happens.

2. *Example answers:* recipes, rules, directions

Test-style questions

1. recount *(**1 mark**)*
2.

discussion text	Details of a friction experiment
explanation text	A traveller's guide to Australia
recount text	Why does rain fall?

*(**2 marks** for all three correct; **1 mark** for one correct.)*

3. *Example answers:* explanation of the water cycle, etc. *(**1 mark** for each suitable answer.)*

Pages 58–59
Practice activity

1. *Example answers:* **species:** a group of living things that have similar characteristics; **southern hemisphere:** the half of the Earth that is south of the equator; **krill:** shrimp-like animals that live in the open sea; **crustaceans:** animals that usually have a hard covering or "exoskeleton", and two pairs of antennae or feelers, e.g. crabs.

Test-style questions

1. Africa; New Zealand *(**1 mark** for circling both correct answers.)*
2. *Example answer:* What penguins eat. *(**1 mark** for a suitable heading that recognises that the paragraph is about what penguins eat.)*
3. They cannot count every penguin in the world. *(**2 marks** for an explanation that shows that every penguin cannot be counted; **1 mark** for an answer that says it is just a guess, without explanation.)*

Pages 60–61
Practice activities

1. A recipe or instruction text. The title, ingredients list and numbered steps show its text type.
2. So that you can identify them quickly and easily when making a shopping list or deciding if you are going to enjoy eating it.

Test-style questions

1. 250 *(**1 mark**)*
2. cool it *(**1 mark**)*
3. 4 *(**1 mark**)*
4. put / bring / stir / remove / cool / tip / make / strain / take / serve *(**1 mark** for one verb written correctly.)*
5. *Example answer:* **Yes**, because I like strawberries and blackberries. *(**2 marks** for an answer using the text; **1 mark** for a plausible answer that does not use the text.)*

Pages 62–63
Practice activities

1. Harry during his record attempt.
2. **Who?** Harry Jones; **What?** balancing doughnuts on his head; **Where?** Barnstaple; **When?** this week; **Why?** to set a world record

Test-style questions

1. 44 *(**1 mark**)*
2. Jones *(**1 mark**)*
3. *Example answer:* A Balancing Act *(**1 mark** for a plausible headline that is linked to the content of the article – it does not have to be funny.)*
4. *Example answers:* **Yes**, it would be good to break Harry's record. Harry practised and persevered and I would want to do this too. **No**, I don't think I could balance more than 44 doughnuts, but I could try balancing something else instead and set a different world record. *(**2 marks** for a plausible explanation based on evidence from the*

*text; **1 mark** for giving a reason that is not based on details from the article.)*

Pages 64–65
Practice activities
1. *Example answers:* **Paragraph 1:** The Solar System; **Paragraph 2:** The Sun; **Paragraph 3:** Mercury
2. seven

Test-style questions
1. 350˚C *(**1 mark**)*
2. elliptical *(**1 mark**)*
3. 88 *(**1 mark**)*
4. *Any **fact** that is about the Sun, taken from the article. (**1 mark**)*

Pages 66–67
Practice activities
1. alphabetically
2. *Example answer:* What equipment do you need? *(Any question – beginning with a capital letter and finishing with a question mark – that would be relevant for the rowing section.)*

Test-style questions
1. 23 *(**1 mark**)*
2. diving *(**1 mark**)*
3. 5–11 year olds *(**1 mark**), because it mentions "school sports" (**1 mark**).*
4. A glossary gives definitions of the technical words in the book. *(**2 marks** for an explanation that states definitions of technical words / vocabulary; **1 mark** for an explanation that only states definitions of words / vocabulary.)*

Pages 68–69
Practice activities
1. bold headings, colour, questions, different sized text, illustration
2. when it is; where it is; what it is

Test-style questions
1. 6 *(**1 mark**)*
2. summer *(**1 mark**)*
3. *Example answers:* Details of more events / cost of activities / age restrictions *(**1 mark** for each relevant idea up to a total of **2 marks**. The information should be **additional** to the poster's content.)*
4. ***Yes** or **No** possible. Children should explain their answer with reference to a feature from the text to gain **1 mark**.*

Pages 70–71
Practice activities
1. **What?** wildlife park; **Where?** heart of England; **Where can you have a hot meal?** Tiger Tavern; **How can you save £2 per person?** book online; **Name four living animals you will see:** *Any four from:* lions, monkeys, wolves, crocodiles, camels and white tigers.
2. *Example answers:* photos, illustrations, bright colours, park map.

Test-style questions
1. High-Wire Tree Adventure *(**1 mark**)*
2. fast food *(**1 mark**)*
3. fantastic / fun / huge / numerous / exciting / brilliant / excellent *(**1 mark** for each correct word, up to a total of **2 marks**.)*

2. Which one of these statements about the poem is **false**?

Tick **one**

Sentences are broken up into separate lines. ☐

It rhymes. ☐

It uses just a few words to describe the scene. ☐

Test-style questions

1. What takes a bow? Circle **one** answer.

winter **autumn** **summer** **spring** *1 mark*

2. What is the word "wings" referring to in this poem?

Tick **one**

a bird's wings ☐

the wings at the edge of a stage ☐

an aeroplane's wings ☐ *1 mark*

3. What are there lines of? Circle **one** answer.

snowdrops **spiderwebs** **puddles** **snow** *1 mark*

4. One season is turning into another. Fill in the blanks to show what is happening.

____________ is turning into ____________ *1 mark*

5. One of the lines says, "Beneath the crystal covering". To what is the poet referring?

____

____

1 mark

Words and phrases in poems

Key to comprehension

Poems often use words and phrases that are more intense and striking than those used in other texts, both in terms of their sound and the images they use.

Phrases are often created to fit a rhythm or a rhyme pattern, and poets sometimes make use of the following techniques:

- Repetition (e.g. tiger, tiger!)
- Alliteration (e.g. creeping cat)
- Simile (e.g. he is like a star)
- Metaphor (e.g. he is a star).

Comprehension material

Weird is the Woman

Weird is the woman who lives in the woods
and weird are the clothes she wears.
Crooked the roof of her gingerbread house
and crooked the rickety stairs.
Tattered and patched are the curtains that hide
the tattered and patched things decaying inside.

Sneaky and cheeky the children who spy,
leaving their safe little homes nearby.
Creaky and squeaky footsteps on the floor,
creaky and squeaky the hinge on the door.
No time to run from what stands there…
a tiny old lady with bugs in her hair.

"Come in my dears, I'm about to have dinner.
I'll disappear if I get any thinner!
I look forward to children coming to snoop,
it gives me something to put in my soup!"

Practice activities

1. Use **two** words from the box to fill in the spaces below.

alliteration	rhyming	repetition	capital letters

At the end of the fifth and sixth lines the poet has used ____________________.

Within these lines she has used ____________________.

2. Which **three** words in the first line make use of alliteration?

______________ ______________ ______________

Test-style questions

1. What did the lady have in her hair? Circle **one** answer.

cobwebs **food** **bugs** **clips** *1 mark*

2. Which word has been used to rhyme with "dinner"?

__________________________ *1 mark*

3. Which two adjectives are repeated in stanza two?

__________________________ and __________________________ *1 mark*

4. Do you like the poem?

YES **NO** (circle **one**)

Explain your answer.

____

____

____

2 marks

Narrative poetry

Key to comprehension

Narrative poems are the oldest form of poetry. They tell stories with a beginning (which introduces the background to the story), a middle (which relates the main events) and an end (which concludes and summarises the story). In times when most people did not read or write, people shared stories verbally and in a style that was almost song-like. Indeed, songs that you hear nowadays are simply poems that have been set to music.

Comprehension material

Extract from "The Pied Piper of Hamelin" by Robert Browning

Hamelin Town's in Brunswick,
By famous Hanover city;
The river Weser, deep and wide,
Washes its walls on either side;
A pleasanter spot you never spied;
But, when begins my ditty*,
Almost five hundred years ago,
To see the townsfolk suffer so
From vermin*, was a pity.

Rats!
They fought the dogs and killed the cats,
And bit the babies in the cradles,
And ate the cheeses out of the vats*,
And licked the soup from the cooks' own ladles,
Split open the kegs of salted sprats*.
Made nests inside men's Sunday hats.
And even spoiled the women's chats
By drowning their speaking
With shrieking and squeaking
In fifty different sharps and flats.

ditty:** *song / poem;* ***vermin: *nuisance animals;* ***vats:*** *containers;* ***sprats:*** *small fish*

Practice activities

1. Which part of the poem is this extract from (the beginning, middle or end)? How do you know?

____

____

2. The author refers to events in the poem that happened how many years ago? Circle **one** answer.

600 years **500 years** **200 years** **100 years**

Test-style questions

1. What does the word "vermin" refer to in this poem? Circle **one** answer.

pipers **children** **adults** **rats** *1 mark*

2. What did the rats do to the men's hats? Circle **one** answer.

split them open **licked soup from them** **made nests in them** **ate them**

1 mark

3. How did the rats spoil the women's chats?

____

____

1 mark

4. Which city is Brunswick near to?

______________________ *1 mark*

5. Which word has been used to rhyme with "ladles"?

______________________ *1 mark*

Forms of poetry

Key to comprehension

Poetry comes in many different **forms**: rhyming poems, narrative poems, acrostic poems, list poems, shape poems, number poems, to mention but a few.

It is important to be able to recognise some of these poems, not just by content, but by form. For instance, a list poem contains a list of things; an acrostic poem spells a word with the first letter of each line; and a narrative poem tells a story.

Comprehension material

School

Starting early;
Cornflakes eaten.
How I wish I could stay in bed!
Once there, I learn to read and write;
Only then will I achieve success.
Learning is so rewarding!

Learning

My mother asked me what I had learned
at school the other day,
I scratched my head and said:
"How to read a book upside down.
How to get second helpings of lunch.
How to talk to my friend without the teacher noticing.
How to copy maths sums from another book.
How to draw funny faces on the bottom of the table.
How to chew gum without being caught.
And, how to wriggle out of trouble."
It is funny that every day this week…
she has not asked me that question again.

Practice activities

1. What type of poem is "School" and how do you know?

____

____

2. What type of poem is "Learning" and how do you know?

____

____

Test-style questions

1. What does the child wish for in "School"?

Tick **one**

to be able to read and write ☐

to be able to stay in bed ☐

to be able to have toast ☐

1 mark

2. What did the child in "Learning" learn to get at lunchtime? Circle **one** answer.

second helpings **detention** **a newspaper** **a football**

1 mark

3. Why might the mother in "Learning" not have asked the same question again?

____

1 mark

4. What might the mother have expected the child to have learned at school?

____

____

2 marks

Key to comprehension

The **main idea** of a text is not just the information from the beginning of the text or paragraph. Neither is it just what the text is about. The main idea is what the author wants the reader to understand as being **important and valued** within the text.

For instance, the first paragraph of a letter should introduce the main and most important idea, the following sentences and paragraphs should then add extra information to this.

Top tip

The main idea the author is trying to get across to the reader is not always stated clearly.

Comprehension material

14 Hazel Court
Cossington
CG4 0NE

The Manager
The Furniture Store
High Street
Cossington
CG1 4BE

1st July

Dear Sir / Madam,

I am writing to complain about the table I bought from you last week, which was delivered to my house yesterday.

Whilst the table itself is very smart and suitable for purpose, I do not think that you are thinking about the environment enough when you are running your company. The wood that the table is made from has, I believe, been logged illegally in Thailand. Do you know that this, whilst keeping your profit high, is threatening the habitats of people and birds, let alone destroying the natural barrier against global warming? I am very worried about the environment but do not think you are.

I feel strongly that you need to think more carefully about how your business is having a bad effect on the environment.

Yours faithfully,

Sam Smith

Practice activities

1. Why is Sam cross?

Tick **one**

He doesn't like the look of the table. ☐

His delivery was late. ☐

He had bad service at the store. ☐

He doesn't think the manager cares about the environment. ☐

2. What, in particular, is Sam concerned about?

____

____

Test-style questions

1. What is the name of the shop that Sam has written to? Circle **one** answer.

The Furniture Store **14 Hazel Court** **Cossington** **The High Street**

1 mark

2. Whose address is in the top right-hand corner? Circle **one** answer.

the Manager's **Sam's** **the shop's** **the table's**

1 mark

3. If you were the manager, what question might you ask Sam in response?

____

____

____

1 mark

Summarising ideas 1

Key to comprehension

It is important to be able to **summarise information** from one or a number of sources, in order to draw out the key points without re-reading everything.

For instance, after an accident or crime, the police sometimes have to collect and study statements from the people who saw it happen (the witnesses).

If you had 20 witness statements about one event, you could pull out the points that are consistent between them and create a **summary** of what occurred, based on the different accounts.

Top tip

Think about each word you write and whether it is absolutely necessary to the summary.

Comprehension material

Witness statement

I was standing by the penguin enclosure at the zoo at about 12.15pm on Saturday. There were people standing all around the walls, as we were waiting for the keepers to come and feed the penguins. I was watching the penguins, which were huddled together on what I believe must be their feeding rock.

Suddenly, my attention was drawn to the other end of the enclosure where a man was shouting at a little girl. He said, "I told you to hold on to it carefully!" The little girl (who was around 9 years old) was crying. It was then that I noticed a camera just below them, in the penguin enclosure.

The man then lifted the little girl up over the small wall and let her down into the penguin enclosure. Lots of people gasped as the signs clearly said, "Do not enter the penguin enclosure." The little girl was no longer crying. Instead of getting the camera, she walked closer to the penguins, which all began to move towards her. She put out her hand to touch one and it nuzzled her hand.

It was at this moment that her dad yelled, "Help! Help! The penguins are attacking my daughter!" The keepers arrived for the feeding and he immediately began shouting at them. One of the keepers dropped into the enclosure, picked up the girl (and the camera) and handed both back to the shouting man.

Practice activities

1. Write three bullets points to list the key information from the first paragraph.

   - **Where:** ______________________
   - **When:** ______________________
   - **Why witness was there:** ______________________

2. Write a summary of what happened in no more than 50 words.

____

____

____

____

Test-style questions

1. What relation was the man to the girl? Circle **one** answer.

   her brother **the zoo keeper** **her dad** **her uncle** *1 mark*

2. Was the girl scared of the penguins? How do you know?

____

____

2 marks

3. Were the penguins attacking the little girl? **YES** **NO** (circle **one**)

   Explain your answer.

____

____

2 marks

Key to comprehension

A useful skill for reading is being able to **scan** longer texts and write notes or bullet points about **key information**.

It can make things clearer in your mind and help in practical ways in everyday life.

For instance, a tourist guide book might give many ideas about things to do on holiday, so writing your own short notes as you read could help.

Comprehension material

A Visitor's Guide to Weymouth, Dorset

The seaside town of Weymouth, in the county of Dorset, is a gateway to the Jurassic Coast. It was originally a fishing village and played a key role in the D-Day invasion.

The Esplanade looks over Weymouth Bay, which is a safe beach with golden sand. The water is clear and shallow so provides the opportunity for safe bathing. The seafront has a wide variety of restaurants, pubs, cafes and small shops.

Even if it is raining, you will never be bored in Weymouth because there are so many interesting places to visit.

The Deep Sea Adventure has a Titanic Exhibition, whilst Sharky's is an indoor children's play zone full of exciting opportunities.

Brewers Quay houses the Timewalk attraction, which explores Weymouth's past, whilst the Nothe Fort Museum of Coastal Defence gives visitors a memorable insight into Weymouth's maritime history.

The Sea Life Park has lots of marine creatures, from seals to sharks and even turtles!

There are also lots of amazing events held in Weymouth throughout the year, including an international kite festival, military parades, volleyball and sailing championships, a carnival in August and a Christmas Day swim in the harbour!

If all that isn't enough, Weymouth even has the best sunshine record in England, even in winter!

Practice activities

1. What county is Weymouth in?

____

2. Write a bullet point list of the places in Weymouth mentioned in the fourth, fifth and sixth paragraphs.

- ____________________
- ____________________
- ____________________
- ____________________
- ____________________

Test-style questions

1. Where can you learn about Weymouth's maritime history? Circle **one** answer.

   Nothe Fort Museum **Sea Life Park** **Brewers Quay** *1 mark*

2. When is there a special swim in the harbour? Circle **one** answer.

   Easter **Christmas** **August** **Summer** *1 mark*

3. What adjective is used to describe the **events** in Weymouth?

   ____________________ *1 mark*

4. If your family was going to Weymouth, write down three places you would like to visit and **why** (based on information given in the guide).

   a) ____________________

   b) ____________________

   c) ____________________

   3 marks

Presentation and meaning 1

Key to comprehension

The way that text is **presented** can signal lots of information to the reader.

For instance, if you glance at a piece of paper and see an address in the top right-hand corner, you know this is likely to be a letter.

Similarly, if you see a text with a big headline and columns of writing underneath it, you think "newspaper".

Presentation can play a key role in how a reader understands a text. You therefore need to be familiar with the standard layout features of different text types.

Comprehension material

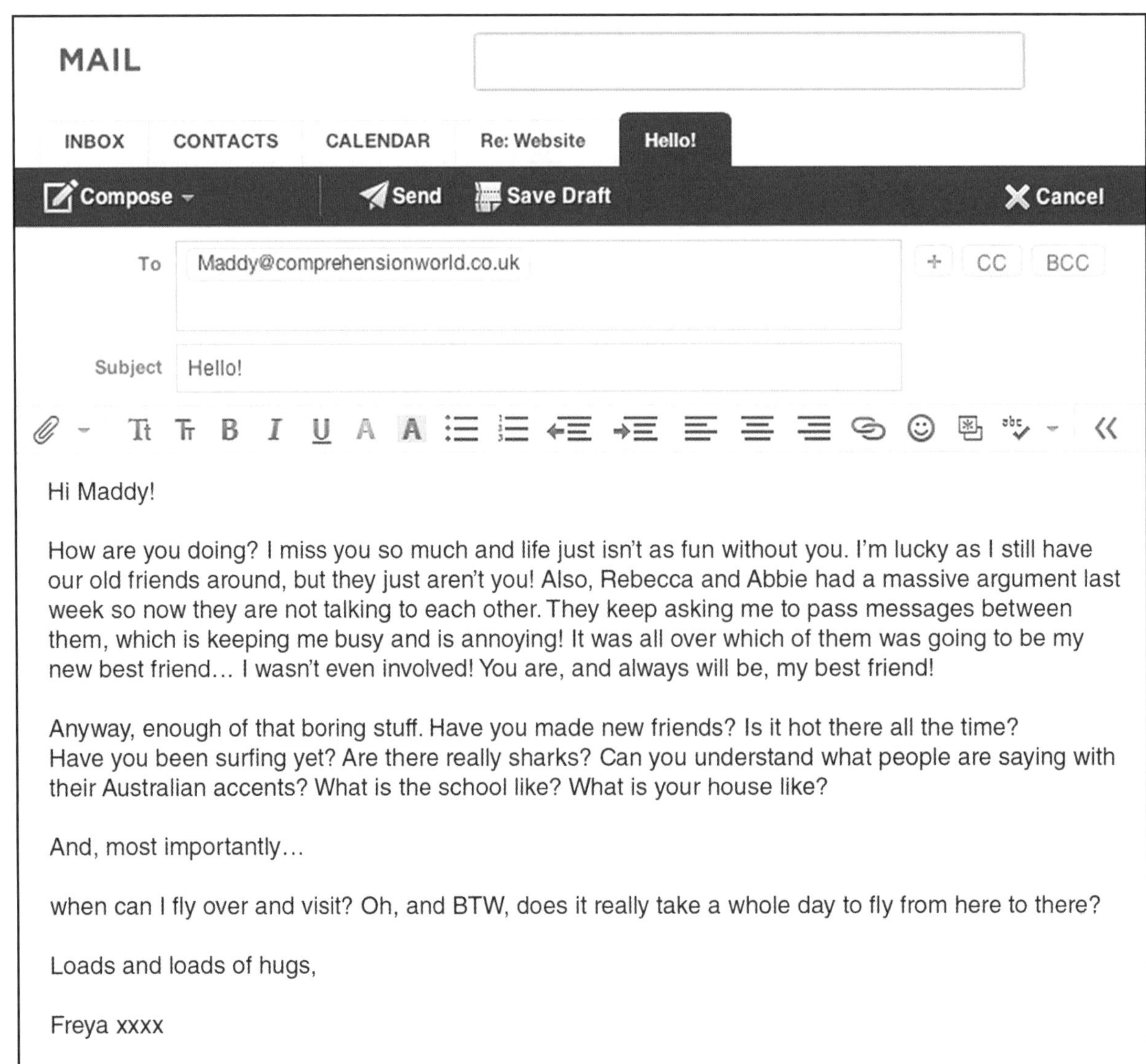

Hi Maddy!

How are you doing? I miss you so much and life just isn't as fun without you. I'm lucky as I still have our old friends around, but they just aren't you! Also, Rebecca and Abbie had a massive argument last week so now they are not talking to each other. They keep asking me to pass messages between them, which is keeping me busy and is annoying! It was all over which of them was going to be my new best friend… I wasn't even involved! You are, and always will be, my best friend!

Anyway, enough of that boring stuff. Have you made new friends? Is it hot there all the time? Have you been surfing yet? Are there really sharks? Can you understand what people are saying with their Australian accents? What is the school like? What is your house like?

And, most importantly…

when can I fly over and visit? Oh, and BTW, does it really take a whole day to fly from here to there?

Loads and loads of hugs,

Freya xxxx

Practice activities

1. What type of text is this? How do you know?

____

____

2. Some informal words and phrases are used in this text that would not be used in a formal letter. Write down three examples of this.

a) ____________ **b)** ____________

c) ____________

Test-style questions

1. Where is Maddy now? Circle **one** answer.

England **America** **Ireland** **Australia** *1 mark*

2. Who had an argument with Abbie? Circle **one** answer.

Freya **Rebecca** **Maddy** **Vicky** *1 mark*

3. "Maddy has gone on holiday." Is this correct? **YES** **NO** (circle **one**)

Explain your answer.

____

2 marks

4. Has Freya agreed to pass messages between the two girls who are arguing?

YES **NO** (circle **one**)

Which words tell you this?

____

2 marks

Structure and meaning 1

Key to comprehension

Text **structure** refers to the way that an author organises the text. This is determined by the type and purpose of the text.

For instance, a formal letter will be structured based on the conventions for this type of text, whilst an explanation text will be structured to help the reader understand and remember information, perhaps using headings, sub-headings, diagrams and bullet points.

Comprehension material

Rain

How does rain form?

Water droplets are formed when warm air (which holds lots of water) rises into the sky and then cools. Water vapour is always in the air – we just can't see it! When enough of the water droplets collect together, they form a cloud. If the clouds grow in size and contain enough water droplets, the droplets knock together and form even bigger drops. When the drops become too heavy, they fall (due to gravity) as rain.

More rain facts:

- Water can also fall from the sky as hail, sleet or snow.
- If rain is particularly heavy, it can cause flooding and landslides.
- We can create electricity using water. This is called **hydropower**.

DID YOU KNOW?

The highest amount of rainfall ever recorded in one year is 25.4m, in Cherrapunji, India.

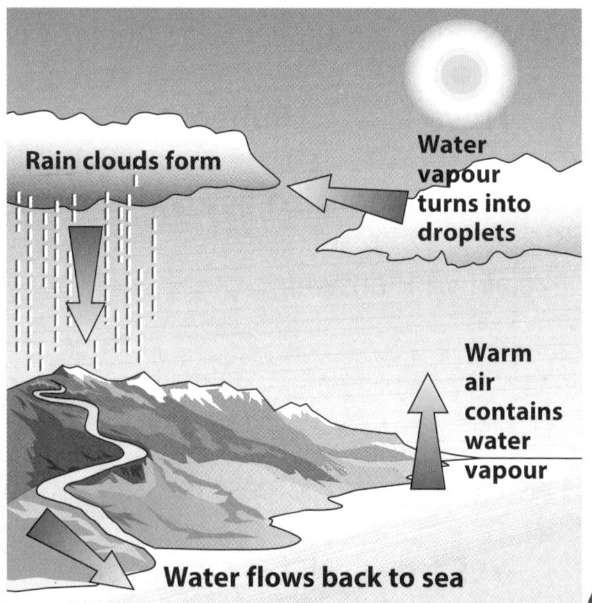

Rain is a key part of the water cycle.

Practice activities

1. Use the words in the box to fill in the spaces below.

author	reader	explanation	sub-headings

The ____________ has used ____________ to help structure this

____________ text and help the ____________ understand it in more detail.

2. How does the diagram help the reader understand the information in the first paragraph better?

____

____

____

Test-style questions

1. What is in the air but cannot be seen? Circle **one** answer.

rain **snow** **water vapour** **hail**

1 mark

2. What is electricity created by water called? Circle **one** answer.

hydropower **hyperpower** **waterpower** **rainpower**

1 mark

3. What do you think **hydro** might mean in the term "hydropower"?

Explain your answer.

____

____

____

2 marks

Language and meaning

Key to comprehension

The **language** that is used in text is determined by the audience and purpose of the text.

For example, if the text is a letter to your teacher, you would use formal language.

In contrast, a diary entry might include informal language, slang terms and abbreviations.

Comprehension material

Dear Diary,

What a wicked day! I went to the beach with my mum, dad, granny, grandpa, uncle, auntie and little cousin. It was so hot that we were able to stay there all day! Grandpa made an amazing sandcastle that was enormous. He even made a ramp so that a ball rolled down from the top to the moat!

My best bit was going in the inflatable boat and being pulled in fast by Daddy so that it felt like a speedboat. Water even came up over the front and into the boat!!

I also loved it when we went to the amusements, even though we didn't win anything! We never do. Well, sometimes Granny wins on the 2p machines, but I never have!

My cousin had this cool bucket thing where you made a little sandcastle using the bucket and then stuck on arms, eyes, ears and other funny stuff (just like my Mr Potato Head). I was quite jealous cos it was fab, but Matilda let me share it, so I still got to play with it loads.

I also collected lots of shells that I'm gonna clean tomorrow, so I can make a pattern with them for my bedroom wall…

Gotta get some sleep now tho cos I've got to go to school tomorrow. Boo!

Practice activities

1. What type of text is this? How do you know?

2. Some informal words are used in this text that would not be used in formal text. Write down three examples of these.

   a) ______ b) ______

   c) ______

Test-style questions

1. Who made an "amazing sandcastle"? Circle **one** answer.

   Matilda **Daddy** **Grandpa** **Granny** *1 mark*

2. What was the author's best bit? Circle **one** answer.

   sandcastles **inflatable boat** **amusements** **shells** *1 mark*

3. Match the person to the action or description that refers to them.

Action or description	Person
wins on 2p machines	Daddy
owns a "cool bucket thing"	Granny
pulled boat in fast	Matilda

2 marks

4. Rewrite the fourth paragraph to make it sound formal.

2 marks

Types of non-fiction text

Key to comprehension

Non-fiction is a type of writing based on real-life events or facts, as opposed to a made-up story (fiction).

There are lots of different forms of non-fiction. When you have identified the text type, you need to think about the **audience** (who the text is aimed at) and the **purpose** (what the text is trying to do).

Top tip

When you first see a text, try to identify its type, audience and purpose.

Comprehension material

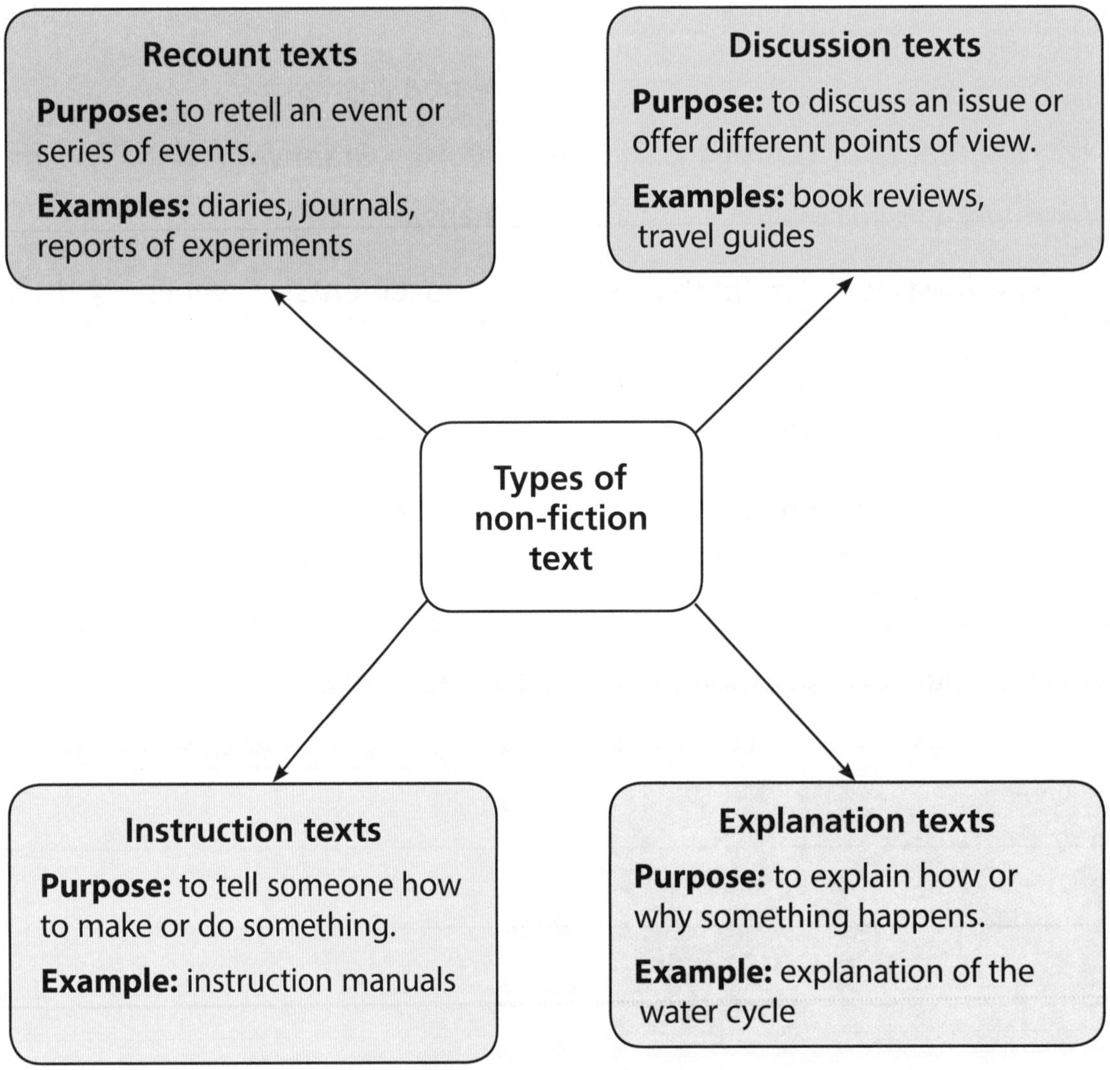

Types of non-fiction text

Recount texts

Purpose: to retell an event or series of events.

Examples: diaries, journals, reports of experiments

Discussion texts

Purpose: to discuss an issue or offer different points of view.

Examples: book reviews, travel guides

Instruction texts

Purpose: to tell someone how to make or do something.

Example: instruction manuals

Explanation texts

Purpose: to explain how or why something happens.

Example: explanation of the water cycle

Practice activities

1. Write down three different "purposes" that non-fiction texts can have.

a) ______________________

b) ______________________

c) ______________________

2. Write down two more examples that could go in the "instruction texts" box, i.e. two other types of text that are instructional.

a) ______________________

b) ______________________

Test-style questions

1. What type of text is a diary? Circle **one** answer.

recount **discussion** **explanation** **persuasive**

1 mark

2. Match the type of text to the example shown.

Type of text
discussion text
explanation text
recount text

Example
Details of a friction experiment
A traveller's guide to Australia
Why does rain fall?

2 marks

3. Write down **two** other topics that might be covered in an explanation text.

a) ______________________

b) ______________________

2 marks

Key to comprehension

All non-fiction text will have some form of **subject-specific vocabulary**.

For instance, text about the Internet will have ICT-specific language, e.g. computer, Internet, modem.

By reading non-fiction texts, you will develop your vocabulary because of these subject-specific words.

Top tip

A glossary in a non-fiction book can help you to understand subject-specific vocabulary.

Comprehension material

Penguins

Penguins are birds that cannot fly. The name "penguin" comes from the Welsh words *pen*, meaning "head", and *gwyn*, meaning "white" – "white head"!

There are 17 species of penguin which are all slightly different from each other. All of the species live in the southern hemisphere, mainly at the South Pole. They can also be found on the coasts of South America, the Galapagos Islands, Australia, Africa and New Zealand. In total, there might be as many as 100 million penguins in the world! Just imagine if they were all huddled together in one place!

Penguins waddle when they walk. They have black and white feathers and a torpedo-shaped body that helps them to speed through the water (they can travel at speeds of up to 25 miles an hour!). Most of the time penguins are in the water looking for food. They are excellent swimmers: they can spin, jump and dive whilst searching for food, but they cannot swim backwards! They can hold their breath underwater for about six minutes. When moving from the water to the land, they can launch themselves six feet into the air.

A penguin's main diet is fish but they also eat squid, krill and crustaceans. They have a hook at the end of their bill which helps them to grab their food. They also have bristles that face backwards on their tongues to stop slippery seafood from getting away. Penguins have a special gland in their bodies that takes the salt out of the seawater they drink, so that they actually drink filtered water!

Practice activity

1. Use a dictionary or another information source to write definitions for the words below.

species: ______________________________

____

southern hemisphere: ______________________________

____

krill: ______________________________

____

crustaceans: ______________________________

____

Test-style questions

1. On which coasts can penguins be found? Circle **two** answers.

Africa **Wales** **New Zealand** **India**

1 mark

2. Write a sub-heading that could be used for the final paragraph.

____

1 mark

3. Why does it only say there "might" be as many as 100 million penguins in the world?

____

____

2 marks

Presentation and meaning 2

Key to comprehension

You can pick up a great deal from text simply by glancing at the way it is presented.

For instance, instructions to make something usually have a list of materials required, followed by numbered steps using imperative verbs (also known as "bossy verbs" – they tell people what to do!) and, sometimes, diagrams.

At a glance, the reader can identify the text as a list of instructions without having to read anything.

Top tip

Learn what the key layout features of each text type are, so you can identify them quickly.

Comprehension material

Frozen fruit sticks with blackberry sauce

Ingredients

For the fruit sticks:
100g strawberries, cut in half
100g mango, cut into chunks
100g melon, cut into chunks
2 kiwi fruits peeled and cut into chunks

For the blackberry sauce:
250g blackberries
50g golden caster sugar
½ teaspoon vanilla extract

Method

1. Put the blackberries and sugar into a small saucepan with 100ml water.
2. Bring to the boil, then simmer for 5 minutes until the fruit is soft.
3. Stir in the vanilla extract, remove and cool a little.
4. Put the fruit on wooden sticks.
5. Put the sticks into the freezer for 1 hour until they are just starting to freeze.
6. Whilst the fruit is in the freezer, tip the contents of the pan into a food processor and make it into a purée.
7. Strain the purée through a sieve to make it smooth.
8. Put into a jug ready to serve.
9. Take the sticks out of the freezer and serve with the sauce.

Practice activities

1. What type of text is this? How do you know?

2. Why do you think the ingredients are listed first?

Test-style questions

1. How many grams of blackberries are needed? Circle **one** answer.

   100 **250** **50** **200** *1 mark*

2. After stirring in the vanilla extract, what do you have to do? Circle **one** answer.

   stir it **eat it** **mix it** **cool it** *1 mark*

3. How many different ingredients are needed to make just the fruit sticks? Circle **one** answer.

   6 **5** **4** **3** *1 mark*

4. Write one **imperative verb** that is used in the text.

   1 mark

5. Would you like to make the fruit sticks?

   YES **NO** (circle **one**)

   Explain your answer using the text.

   2 marks

Key to comprehension

Non-fiction texts are **structured** based on their purpose (the reason why they are written), as well as taking into account the audience (who they are written for).

For instance, a newspaper report often has a headline, a picture with a caption and then a report written in columns. The first paragraph often answers the basic questions: who, what, where, when and why?

Top tip

Have a look in a newspaper and try to identify headings, sub-headings, columns, pictures and captions.

Comprehension material

Doughnut-tastic!

It is quite common to read about children's sporting and academic achievements. However, a child achieving a world record in balancing doughnuts on his head is almost unheard of. But that is what Harry Jones from Barnstaple received an award for this week.

The award was given to the 14 year old by the Guinness World Records team when they arrived in Barnstaple to verify his unusual claims. Harry had been working at the record since the age of 10, when he became obsessed with the little, round, sugary treats! While other youngsters spent their free time at the park, watching TV, or playing on games consoles, Harry saved his pocket money to buy doughnuts to balance on his head. He soon realised that he needed a trusty companion to help him to reach his goal. This is when he gave the important role of "doughnut support person" to his older brother.

By the age of 12 he was able to balance 12 doughnuts on his head; by the age of 13 he had doubled this to 24 doughnuts; and by the time he reached 14, when he was ready to have his record verified, he could balance an amazing 44 doughnuts on top of his head.

Speaking of his achievement, he said, "I am happy with it for now as it has set a baseline for the record. I still want to go further, or even try balancing different things on my head."

Watch this space for what he is going to attempt next!

Harry during his record attempt

Practice activities

1. Write the words that make up the caption in this report.

____

2. Write the answers to the following questions about this article:

Who? ____________________ **What?** ____________________

Where? ____________________ **When?** ____________________

Why? ____________________

Test-style questions

1. How many doughnuts could Harry balance on his head when he was 14? Circle **one** answer.

14 **12** **44** **24** *1 mark*

2. What is Harry's surname? Circle **one** answer.

Smith **Jones** **Harry** **Barnstaple** *1 mark*

3. Write an alternative headline for this article.

____

1 mark

4. Would you like to attempt this record? **YES** **NO** (circle **one**)

Explain your answer with clear reasons, based on details in the report.

____

____

____

2 marks

Structure of non-fiction texts

Key to comprehension

The way that non-fiction text is structured helps the reader to understand it.

Paragraphs are a great tool for doing this as they allow the writer to break the text up into smaller sections that focus on different ideas.

Sub-headings can also be added to the start of each paragraph to signal what the paragraph is about.

Comprehension material

Outer Space

The Solar System is the name that we give to the Sun and everything that travels around it. This includes the eight main planets – Mercury, Venus, Earth, Mars, Jupiter, Saturn, Uranus, Neptune – and their moons. It also includes dwarf planets, such as Pluto, and their moons, as well as comets and asteroids and other objects such as satellites and rubbish from spacecraft. The path of a planet around the Sun is called its orbit. The orbits of the planets are not circles but ellipses (oval shapes).

The Sun is about 4,600,000,000 years old and has a diameter of about 1,392,500 kilometres. If you imagine the Earth is the size of a golf ball, then in comparison the Sun would be the size of a beachball! The surface temperature of the Sun is about 5,500°C. It takes just over 8 minutes for the rays from the Sun to reach us on Earth, although we only receive a tiny fraction of the energy that the Sun gives out.

Mercury is closest to the Sun, which makes it hard for us to see it. It can reach a temperature of 350°C during the day, making it impossible for life to exist there. At night it drops to below –170°C! Whilst it takes 365.25 days (one year) for the Earth to travel around the Sun, it only takes 88 days for Mercury to travel around the Sun as it is so much closer to it.

Practice activities

1. Write a sub-heading that could be used for each paragraph.

   Paragraph 1 ______________________________

   Paragraph 2 ______________________________

   Paragraph 3 ______________________________

2. If a paragraph was needed for each of the main planets, how many more paragraphs would be needed?

   ____

Test-style questions

1. What temperature can it reach on Mercury in the daytime? Circle **one** answer.

   –170°C **350°C** **365.25°C** **88°C**

   1 mark

2. What shape are the orbits of the planets? Circle **one** answer.

   cuboidical **spherical** **eggitical** **elliptical**

   1 mark

3. How many days would one year be on Mercury? Circle **one** answer.

   365.25 **350** **88** **5500**

   1 mark

4. Copy **one fact** from the report about the Sun.

   ____

   ____

   1 mark

Key to comprehension

When reading, it is important to **ask questions** about the text to ensure that you are fully engaged with it. You need to think about what the author wants the reader to understand. As the reader, you need to ask questions, such as:

- Why has the author chosen to write in this way?
- Who is the text aimed at?
- How is it organised?

Top tip

Look at the contents page of a book to help you find your way around it.

Comprehension material

Contents

Practice activities

1. In what order are the sports listed in this book?

____

2. Write a question that could be answered in the rowing pages.

____

Test-style questions

1. To which page should you turn to learn about a game that uses a net, rackets and a small, yellow ball? Circle **one** answer.

21 **19** **25** **23** *1 mark*

2. What can you learn about on page 9? Circle **one** answer.

diving **swimming** **archery** **basketball** *1 mark*

3. Which group of people do you think the book is for?

	Tick **one**
0–4 year olds	☐
5–11 year olds	☐
Adults	☐

Explain your answer.

____

2 marks

4. What is a glossary (page 32) for?

____

2 marks

Key to comprehension

To be a good reader you need to be able to **skim** read (look quickly through the text without reading every part) and identify the key information.

This is what advertising and public notices such as posters, road signs, flyers, etc. rely upon. They are designed to be read quickly (maybe from a car) and need to get the information across to the reader quickly.

You need to be able to skim the text and understand the information at speed.

Comprehension material

Brookside School
Family Fun Day

WHEN?
3rd August between 10am and 4pm

WHERE?
Brookside School grounds

WHAT?
Circus skills, BBQ, pony rides, face painting, ice creams, competitions, raffles and…

… much, much more!

Brighten up your holiday by coming to our special event!

Check the school website for more details

Practice activities

1. How does the text make the main information stand out?

2. What three main pieces of information does the poster give?

   a)

   b)

   c)

Test-style questions

1. How many hours does the event last? Circle **one** answer.

   4 **5** **6** **10** *1 mark*

2. What time of year does the event take place in? Circle **one** answer.

   autumn **summer** **spring** **winter** *1 mark*

3. What other information might be on the website that is not on the poster?

   2 marks

4. Do you think this poster is good for giving information?

   Explain your answer.

   1 mark

Retrieving information 2

Key to comprehension

The way in which information is provided depends on the purpose and the audience. The author needs to think about how long the reader has to **take in** the information. For example, an advert by the side of the road has to communicate information quickly to people passing by, whereas a leaflet (which can be picked up and taken away) can give more detailed information, although it still needs to be eye-catching.

Top tip

Read the wording in leaflets, rather than just looking at the pictures, as this is where the important information is!

Comprehension material

WHAT IS BOWLER'S?

Bowler's Wildlife Park offers a fantastic, fun day out in the heart of England. There is so much to ZOO! We have a huge range of animals, including lions, monkeys, wolves, crocodiles, camels and even WHITE TIGERS! As well as the animals, we have an Indoor Playbarn, Woodland Railway, Safari Ride, Dinosaur Kingdom and – NEW FOR THIS YEAR – a High-Wire Tree Adventure!

FOOD AND DRINK

Bowler's has a huge selection of places to eat and drink: Tiger Tavern offers a range of hot and cold meals for the whole family; Crocodile Creek provides snacks and fast food; and numerous stalls around the park offer drinks, ice cream and other exciting treats. In fact, EVERYTHING you need for a brilliant day out is here!

HOW DO WE GET TO BOWLER'S?

Bowler's is situated just off the M5 at Junction 2. Use the postcode DY2 5HG if using a satnav. There is a bus station 2 minutes' walk from the wildlife park entrance. It has excellent rail routes – check the rail network's website for details.

BOOK ONLINE AND SAVE £2 PER PERSON.

Practice activities

1. Summarise the key information from the leaflet.

   What is Bowler's? ______________________________

   Where is it? ______________________________

Where can you have a hot meal? ______________________

How can you save £2 per person? ______________________

Name four living animals you will see. ______________________

____

2. This extract shows only the words from the leaflet. What else might the leaflet include?

____

____

Test-style questions

1. What is new for this year?

	Tick **one**
High-Wire Tree Adventure	☐
Dinosaur Kingdom	☐
Woodland Railway	☐
white tigers	☐

1 mark

2. What does it say Crocodile Creek offers? Circle **one** answer.

crocodiles **fast food** **ice cream** **fun**

1 mark

3. Write down **two** different adjectives that are used to make the park sound appealing.

______________________ ______________________

2 marks

Acknowledgements

The author and publisher are grateful to the copyright holders for permission to use quoted materials and images.

P04 from *Swallows and Amazons* by *Arthur Ransome*, published by *Jonathan Cape*, reprinted by permission of The Random House Group Limited; except in the U.S.A.: reprinted by permission of David R. Godine, Publisher, Inc. © 1930 by Arthur Ransome; P16 "The Midas Touch" adapted with the kind permission of Mythweb (http://www.mythweb.com); P20 from THE LION, THE WITCH AND THE WARDROBE by C.S. Lewis, copyright © C.S. Lewis Pte. Ltd. 1950. Extract reprinted by permission; P24 from *Grimble* by Clement Freud, reproduced with the kind permission of the Estate of Clement Freud; P26 "The Lion and the Mouse" adapted with the kind permission of Alison Head; P28 "Shipwreck", P36 "On with the Show", P38 "Weird is the Woman" reproduced with the kind permission of Alison Head.

All images are ©Shutterstock, ©Jupiterimages, ©Thinkstock or ©Letts Educational, an imprint of HarperCollins*Publishers* Ltd

Every effort has been made to trace copyright holders and obtain their permission for the use of copyright material. The author and publisher will gladly receive information enabling them to rectify any error or omission in subsequent editions All facts are correct at time of going to press.

Published by Letts Educational
An imprint of HarperCollins*Publishers* Ltd
1 London Bridge Street
London SE1 9GF

ISBN 9780008294168

First published 2013

This edition published 2018

10 9 8 7 6 5 4 3 2

British Library Cataloguing in Publication Data.

A CIP record of this book is available from the British Library.

Commissioning Editor: Tammy Poggo
Author: Rachel Axten-Higgs
Project Editors: Daniel Dyer and Shelley Teasdale
Cover Design: Paul Oates
Inside Concept Design: Ian Wrigley
Layout: Jouve India Private Limited
Production: Natalia Rebow
Printed and bound in Great Britain by Martins the Printers

CGP

Edexcel International GCSE

Mathematics

For the Grade 9-1 Course

The Answer Book

Contents

Published by CGP

ISBN: 978 1 78294 673 1

www.cgpbooks.co.uk

Printed by Elanders Ltd, Newcastle upon Tyne.
Clipart from Corel®

Answers: P1 — P7

Section One — Numbers

Page 1 — Order of Operations

Q1 **a)** 8 **b)** 5 **c)** 6.56 **d)** 11.22 **e)** –0.90 **f)** 319.98 **g)** 5.5 **h)** 983 **i)** 9.17 **j)** 0

Q2 **a)** 8 **b)** 73 **c)** 113 **d)** 7 **e)** 22.57 **f)** 8.67 **g)** 1 **h)** 1.42 **i)** –488.76 **j)** –0.26

Q3 **a)** 3 **b)** 0.1 **c)** 16 **d)** 8.33 **e)** –0.01 **f)** 70.88 **g)** –176.95 **h)** 0.21 **i)** 0.58 **j)** 0.27 **k)** 0.01 **l)** –10.64

Page 2 — Types of Number

Q1 4

Q2 –3 °C

Q3 **a)** 6 ÷ 2 = 3, rational
b) $\sqrt{16}$ = 4, rational
c) $\sqrt{5}$ = 2.23606..., irrational
d) 3 ÷ 8 = 0.375, rational
e) $\sqrt[3]{25}$ = 2.92401..., irrational
f) Rational

Q4 **a)** the third cube number (27)
b) the fourth square number (16)

Q5 **a)** 2
b) e.g. 29
c) 19
d) 19 and 2
e) e.g. 1 or 25

Q6 **a)**

1	**(2)**	**(3)**	4	**(5)**	6	**(7)**	8	9	10
(11)	12	**(13)**	14	15	16	**(17)**	18	**(19)**	20
21	22	**(23)**	24	25	26	27	28	**(29)**	30
(31)	32	33	34	35	36	**(37)**	38	39	40
(41)	42	**(43)**	44	45	46	**(47)**	48	49	50
51	52	**(53)**	54	55	56	57	58	**(59)**	60
(61)	62	63	64	65	66	**(67)**	68	69	70
(71)	72	**(73)**	74	75	76	77	78	**(79)**	80
81	82	**(83)**	84	85	86	87	88	**(89)**	90
91	92	93	94	95	96	**(97)**	98	99	100

b) 3 of: 11 (11), 13 (31), 17 (71), 37 (73), 79 (97)
c) e.g. 3 is a factor of 27

Q7 113

Q8 There's just one: 2 is the only even prime.

Page 3 — Square Roots and Cube Roots

Q1 **a)** 7.7 **b)** 4.4 **c)** 5.8 **d)** 14.1 **e)** 22.8 **f)** 8.7 **g)** 27.4 **h)** 0.9 **i)** 13.0 **j)** 85.0 **k)** 1000.0 **l)** 5.2

Q2 **a)** 2 and –2 **b)** 4 and –4 **c)** 3 and –3 **d)** 7 and –7 **e)** 5 and –5 **f)** 10 and –10 **g)** 12 and –12 **h)** 8 and –8 **i)** 9 and –9

Q3 **a)** 16 **b)** 12 **c)** 11 **d)** 100 **e)** 1 **f)** 0.5

Q4 **a)** 4 **b)** 8 **c)** 5 **d)** 10 **e)** 6 **f)** 20

Q5 7 cm

Q6 240 m

Q7 4

Pages 4-5 — Multiples, Factors and Prime Factors

Q1 **a)** 12
b) 3
c) 1, 9
d) 1, 3, 9
e) P = 12, Q = 6

Q2 Any 5 of:
2 groups of 24, 3 groups of 16, 4 groups of 12, 6 groups of 8, 8 groups of 6, 12 groups of 4, 16 groups of 3, 24 groups of 2.

Q3 The Conversational French and Woodturning classes both have a prime number of pupils and so cannot be divided into equal groups.

Q4 **a)** 1, 8, 27, 64, 125
b) 8, 64
c) 27
d) 8, 64
e) 125

Q5 **a)** 2×3^2
b) $2^2 \times 5 \times 7$
c) 47

Q6 **a)** 2, 3, 5, 7, 11
b) 28
c) $2^2 \times 7$

Q7 **a)** 1, 3, 5, 7, 9
b) 25
c) 5^2

Q8 **a)** 495
b) $3 \times 5 \times 11$

Q9 **a)** 1, 4, 9, 16, 25, 36, 49, 64, 81, 100
b) 4, 16, 36, 64, 100
c) 9, 36, 81
d) 1, 64
e) Total = 385 = 5 × 7 × 11

Q10 **a)** 50 × 25 × 16 = 20,000 cm^3
b) $2^5 \times 5^4$
c) 200. It is not enough to divide the large volume by the smaller volume as the shapes of the blocks are important too. It is possible to fit 16 ÷ 4 = 4 small blocks across the width, 50 ÷ 5 = 10 small blocks along the length and 25 ÷ 5 = 5 small blocks down the height of the large block. This enables Gordon to fit 4 × 10 × 5 = 200 small blocks into the big block.

Q11 **a)** 680
b) $2^2 \times 5 \times 17$
c) $2 \times 5 \times 17$
d) 5×17

Q12 42

Page 6 — LCM and HCF

Q1 **a)** 6, 12, 18, 24, 30, 36, 42, 48, 54, 60
b) 5, 10, 15, 20, 25, 30, 35, 40, 45, 50
c) 30

Q2 **a)** 1, 2, 3, 5, 6, 10, 15, 30
b) 1, 2, 3, 4, 6, 8, 12, 16, 24, 48
c) 6

Q3 **a)** 20 **b)** 10 **c)** 2 **d)** 15 **e)** 15 **f)** 5 **g)** 32 **h)** 16 **i)** 16

Q4 **a)** 120 **b)** 120 **c)** 120 **d)** 45 **e)** 90 **f)** 180 **g)** 64 **h)** 192 **i)** 192

Q5 **a)** $15 = 3 \times 5$
$18 = 2 \times 3^2$
b) $2 \times 3 \times 3 \times 5 = 90$

Q6 **a)** $90 = 2 \times 3^2 \times 5$
$120 = 2^3 \times 3 \times 5$
b) $2 \times 3 \times 5 = 30$

Q7 **a)** $2^4 \times 3^2 = 144$
b) $2^2 \times 3^2 \times 5 \times 7 = 1260$

Q8 **a)** $2 \times 3 \times 5 = 30$
b) $2^2 \times 5 = 20$

Q9 **a)** 7th June (i.e. 6 days later, since 6 is the LCM of 2 and 3)
b) 16th June (i.e. 15 days later, since 15 is the LCM of 3 and 5)
c) Sunday (30 days later, since 30 is the LCM of 2, 3 and 5 — i.e. 4 weeks and 2 days later)
d) Lars (it's 14 days after 1st June, and 14 is a multiple of 2 but not 3 and 5)

Q10 HCF of 36, 42 and 84 is 6.
36 ÷ 6 = 6, 42 ÷ 6 = 7, 84 ÷ 6 = 14
6 + 7 + 14 = 27 friends

Pages 7-9 — Fractions

Q1 **a)** $\frac{1}{64}$ **b)** $\frac{1}{9}$ **c)** $\frac{1}{18}$ **d)** $3\frac{29}{32}$ **e)** $5\frac{5}{32}$ **f)** $\frac{81}{100\,000}$

Q2 **a)** 1 **b)** 4 **c)** $\frac{1}{2}$ **d)** $\frac{2}{5}$ **e)** $\frac{10}{33}$ **f)** 1000

Q3 **a)** $\frac{1}{4}$ **b)** $\frac{5}{6}$ **c)** $\frac{1}{2}$ **d)** $4\frac{3}{8}$ **e)** $5\frac{3}{8}$ **f)** 1

Q4 $3\frac{7}{15}$, so the bowl will be big enough.

Q5 **a)** 0 **b)** $\frac{1}{2}$ **c)** $-\frac{1}{6}$ **d)** $1\frac{7}{8}$ **e)** $-3\frac{1}{8}$ **f)** $\frac{4}{5}$

Answers: P7 — P18

Q6 **a)** $\frac{3}{4}$ **b)** $\frac{5}{12}$ **c)** $\frac{7}{15}$
d) $4\frac{3}{4}$ **e)** 4 **f)** $1\frac{1}{5}$
g) $\frac{5}{8}$ **h)** $-\frac{1}{24}$ **i)** $4\frac{3}{5}$
j) $1\frac{1}{30}$ **k)** 1 **l)** $\frac{44}{75}$

Q7 **a)** 1/12 **b)** 1/4 **c)** 2/3
Q8 **a)** 3/4 of the programme
b) 5/8 of the programme
c) 1/8 of the programme
Q9 3/5 of the kitchen staff are girls.
2/5 of the employees are boys.
Q10 7/30 of those asked had no opinion.
Q11 **a)** 12/30 = 2/5
b) 6 days
Q12 **a)** Each box will hold 16 sandwiches. So 5 boxes will be needed for 80 sandwiches.
b) 25 inches tall

Q13 **a)** $\frac{1}{18}$ **b)** $\frac{1}{4}$
Q14 **a)** 48 km^2 **b)** $\frac{5}{8}$
Q15 **a)** 8 people **b)** $\frac{7}{20}$
c) $\frac{1}{4}$ **d)** 57 people
e) 65 people
Q16 After the 1st bounce the ball reaches 4 m, after the 2nd $2\frac{2}{3}$ m, after the 3rd $1\frac{7}{9}$ m.
Q17 **a)** 100 g flour **b)** 350 g
c) $\frac{2}{7}$ **d)** 300 g
Q18 £31.06

Pages 10-11 — Fractions, Decimals and Percentages

Q1 **a)** 25% **e)** 41.52%
b) 50% **f)** 84.06%
c) 75% **g)** 39.62%
d) 10% **h)** 28.28%
Q2 **a)** 0.5 **e)** 0.602
b) 0.12 **f)** 0.549
c) 0.4 **g)** 0.431
d) 0.34 **h)** 0.788
Q3 **a)** 50% **e)** 4%
b) 25% **f)** 66.7%
c) 12.5% **g)** 26.7%
d) 75% **h)** 28.6%
Q4 **a)** 1/4 **e)** 41/500
b) 3/5 **f)** 62/125
c) 9/20 **g)** 443/500
d) 3/10 **h)** 81/250
Q5 85%
Q6 Grade 6
Q7 **a)** 0.3 **e)** 1.75
b) 0.37 **f)** 0.125
c) 0.4 **g)** 0.6
d) 0.375 **h)** 0.05
Q8

0.5	0.2	0.125	1.6	0.25	3.5	0.15	0.45
1/2	1/5	1/8	8/5	1/4	7/2	3/20	9/20

Q9 **a)** $0.8\dot{3}$ **e)** $0.\dot{9}\dot{0}$
b) $0.\dot{7}$ **f)** $0.\dot{4}6031\dot{7}$
c) $0.\dot{6}\dot{3}$ **g)** $0.\dot{4}7\dot{8}$
d) $0.\dot{4}\dot{7}$ **h)** $0.\dot{5}89\dot{1}$
Q10 **a)** $\frac{3}{5}$ **e)** $\frac{1}{3}$
b) $\frac{3}{4}$ **f)** $\frac{2}{3}$
c) $\frac{19}{20}$ **g)** $\frac{1}{9}$
d) $\frac{16}{125}$ **h)** $\frac{16}{99}$
Q11 **a)** $\frac{2}{9}$ **e)** $\frac{4}{33}$
b) $\frac{4}{9}$ **f)** $\frac{545}{999}$
c) $\frac{8}{9}$ **g)** $\frac{251}{333}$
d) $\frac{80}{99}$ **h)** $\frac{52}{333}$

Pages 12-14 — Percentages

Q1 **a)** £1.28 **b)** 629 kg
c) 16 mins
Q2 **a)** 0.2 **c)** 0.02
b) 0.35 **d)** 0.625
Q3 **a)** $\frac{1}{5}$ **c)** $\frac{7}{10}$
b) $\frac{3}{100}$ **d)** $\frac{421}{500}$
Q4 **a)** 12.5% **c)** 30%
b) 23% **d)** 34%
Q5 85%
Q6 72.5%
Q7 **a)** £4275 **b)** £6840
Q8 1.6%
Q9 500%
Q10 £358.80
Q11 £244.40
Q12 23 028
Q13 Car 1 costs £8495 – (0.15 × £8495)
= £8495 – £1274.25 = £7220.75.
Car 2 costs £8195 – (0.12 × £8195)
= £8195 – £983.40 = £7211.60.
So car 2 is the cheapest.
Q14 £5980
Q15 £152.75, So NO, he couldn't afford it.
Q16 31%
Q17 13%
Q18 **a)** 67.7% **b)** 93.5%
c) 38.1%
Q19 £80
Q20 **a)** 300 **b)** 4 whole years
Q21 £236.25
Q22 38%
Q23 Final cost of stereo
$= x \times (1 + 0.35) \times (1 - 0.2) = x \times 1.08$
So, the shop's overall profit is 8%.
Q24 House value now
$= y \times (1 + 0.1) \times (1 - 0.05)$
$= y \times 1.045$
So, if they sell now they will make a profit of 4.5%.

Page 15 — Interest and Depreciation

Q1 **a)** £473.47 **c)** £779.42
b) £612.52 **d)** £1065
Q2 Splitting the investment. £2.21 better.
Q3 **a)** £7877.94 **d)** £10 646.54
b) £27 116.06 **e)** £7184.25
c) £9980.90 **f)** £5843.70
Q4 **a)** 4% compound interest gives £1040
5% simple interest gives £1050
£5 a month gives £1060
£5 a month account pays more.
b) 4% compound interest gives £4440.73
5% simple interest gives £4500
£5 a month gives £3600
5% simple interest pays more.
c) 4% compound interest gives £5864.84
5% simple interest gives £4950
£5 a month gives £3700
4% compound interest pays more.
Q5 **a)** £270 **d)** £8012
b) £790 **e)** £5100
c) £1130

Pages 16-17 — Ratios

Q1 **a)** 3:4 **d)** 9:16
b) 1:4 **e)** 7:2
c) 1:2 **f)** 9:1
Q2 **a)** 6 cm **d)** 1.5 cm
b) 11 cm **e)** 2.75 cm
c) 30.4 m **f)** 7.6 m
Q3 **a)** £8, £12
b) 80 m, 70 m
c) 100 g, 200 g, 200 g.
d) 1hr 20 m, 2 hr 40 m, 4 hrs.
Q4 John 4, Peter 12
Q5 400 ml, 600 ml, 1000 ml
Q6 30
Q7 Jane £40, Holly £48, Rosemary £12
Q8 £12
Q9 **a)** 245 girls **b)** 210 boys
Q10 **a)** £39 **b)** £140
Q11 **a)** 1:300 **b)** 6 m
c) 3.3 cm
Q12 **a)** 15 kg **b)** 30 kg
c) 8 kg cement, 24 kg sand and 48 kg gravel.
Q13 **a)** 30 fine **b)** 15 not fine
c) 30/45 = 2/3
Q14 **a)** 45 Salt & Vinegar
b) 90 bags sold altogether

Page 18 — Proportion

Q1 85
Q2 £247.80
Q3 112 hrs
Q4 £96.10
Q5 96 sheep
Q6 **a)** 9.33 cm **b)** 30.45 km
Q7 **a)** 400 g
b) 300 g

Answers: P18 — P26

c) She will need 350 g of butter so she doesn't have enough.
d) 4

Q8 44 cows

Q9 a) 55.3 cm c) 20.4 °C
b) 51.5 cm d) 19.5 °C

Pages 19-20 — Rounding Numbers

Q1 a) 62.2 b) 62.19
c) 62.194 d) 19.62433
e) 6.300 f) 3.142

Q2 a) 1330 b) 1330
c) 1329.6 d) 100
e) 0.02 f) 0.02469

Q3 a) 457.0 b) 456.99
c) 456.987 d) 457
e) 460 f) 500

Q4 2.83

Q5 a) 0.704 (to 3 s.f. — the least number of significant figures used in the question).
b) 3.25 (to 3 s.f. — the least number of significant figures used in the question).

Q6 a) £1100 d) £3
b) £88 e) £376
c) £300 f) £44

Q7 23 kg

Q8 £5.07

Q9 235 km

Q10 £19

Q11 £4.77

Q12 235 cm

Q13 470 cm

Q14 1810 g

Q15 13 s

Page 21 — Estimating

Q1 Mark's tank is approximately 4500 cm^3, so it won't be big enough.

Q2 a) 6500 × 2 = 13 000
b) 8000 × 1.5 = 12 000
c) 40 × 1.5 × 5 = 300
d) 45 ÷ 9 = 5
e) 35 000 ÷ 7000 = 5
f) $\frac{55 \times 20}{10} = 55 \times 2 = 110$
g) 7000 × 2 = 14 000
h) 100 × 2.5 × 2 = 500
i) 20 × 20 × 20 = 8000
j) 8000 ÷ 80 = 100
k) 62 000 ÷ 1000 = 62
l) 3 ÷ 3 = 1

Q3 Approximately 15 000 – (1500 + 2500 + 1500 + 1500 + 3000) = 5000

Q4 a) $\frac{150+50}{150-50} = \frac{200}{100} = 2$
b) $\frac{20 \times 10}{\sqrt{400}} = \frac{200}{20} = 10$
c) $\frac{2000 \times 4}{20 \times 5} = \frac{8000}{100} = 80$
d) $\frac{10^2 \div 10}{4 \times 5} = \frac{10}{20} = 0.5$

Q5 a) 2 × (3 × 3) + 2 × (2 × 3.5) = 36 m^2
b) 3 tins

Q6 a) 6.9 (accept 6.8)
b) 10.9 (accept 10.8)
c) 9.2 (accept 9.1)
d) 4.1 (accept 4.2)
e) 9.9 (accept 9.8)
f) 5.8 (accept 5.9)

Pages 22-23 — Bounds

Q1 a) 64.785 kg b) 64.775 kg

Q2 a) 1.75 m
b) 1.85 × 0.75 = 1.3875 m^2

Q3 a) 2.525 l b) 2.475 l

Q4 a) 95 g
b) Upper bound = 97.5 g, lower bound = 92.5 g
c) No, since the lower bound for the electronic scales is 97.5 g, which is greater than the upper bound for the scales in part **a)**.

Q5 a) Upper bound = 13.5, lower bound = 12.5
b) Upper bound = 12.55, lower bound = 12.45
c) To calculate the upper bound for C multiply the upper bound for A by the upper bound for B;
13.5×12.55 = 169.425
To calculate the lower bound for C multiply the lower bound for A by the lower bound for B;
12.5×12.45 = 155.625

Q6 a) Upper bound = 5 minutes 32.5 seconds, lower bound = 5 minutes 27.5 seconds.
b) The lower bound for Jimmy's time is 5 minutes 25 seconds, which is lower than the lower bound for Douglas' time (5 minutes 25.5 seconds).

Q7 a) Upper bound = 945, lower bound = 935.
b) Upper bound = 5.565, lower bound = 5.555.
c) To find the upper bound for R, divide the upper bound for S by the lower bound for T;
945 ÷ 5.555 = 170.117...
To find the lower bound for R, divide the lower bound for S by the upper bound for T;
935÷5.565 = 168.014...
d) 940÷5.56 = 170 (to 2 s.f. — the upper and lower bounds both round to 170 to 2 s.f., but give different answers to 3 s.f.).

Q8 At least 18.2 m^2

Q9 The upper bound for the distance is 127.5 km. The lower bound for the time is 1 hour and 45 minutes = 1.75 hours. The maximum value of the average speed is 127.5÷1.75 = 72.857... km/hour.

Q10 a) Perimeter = 2(12 + 4) = 32 cm.
Maximum possible error = 4 × 0.1 cm = 0.4 cm.
b) Maximum possible error in P is $2(x + y)$.

Pages 24-25 — Standard Form

Q1 a) 35.6 b) 3560
c) 0.356 d) 35600
e) 8.2 f) 0.00082
g) 0.82 h) 0.0082
i) 1570 j) 0.157
k) 157000 l) 15.7

Q2 a) 2.56×10^0 b) 2.56×10
c) 2.56×10^{-1} d) 2.56×10^4
e) 9.52×10 f) 9.52×10^{-2}
g) 9.52×10^4 h) 9.52×10^{-4}
i) 4.2×10^3 j) 4.2×10^{-3}
k) 4.2×10 l) 4.2×10^2

Q3 a) 3.47×10^2 b) 7.3004×10
c) 5×10^0 d) 9.183×10^5
e) 1.5×10^7 f) 9.371×10^6
g) 7.5×10^{-5} h) 5×10^{-4}
i) 5.34×10^0 j) 6.2103×10^2
k) 1.49×10^4 l) 3×10^{-7}

Q4 6×10^{-3}

Q5 1×10^9, 1×10^{12}

Q6 9.46×10^{12}

Q7 6.9138×10^4

Q8 1.2×10^{-2} (mm)

Q9 a) Mercury
b) Jupiter
c) Mercury
d) Neptune
e) Venus and Mercury
f) Jupiter, Neptune and Saturn

Q10 a) 6×10^9 e) 5.6×10^{16}
b) 1.89×10^7 f) 3.99×10^4
c) 4×10^4 g) 4.3473×10^6
d) 2×10^2 h) 1.748×10^4

Q11 a) 2.4×10^{10}
b) 1.6×10^6
c) 1.8×10^5

Q12 1.04×10^{13} is greater by 5.78×10^{12}

Q13 1.3×10^{-9} is smaller by 3.07×10^{-8}

Q14 a) 4.2×10^7 b) 3.8×10^{-4}
c) 1.0×10^7 d) 1.12×10^{-4}
e) 8.43×10^5 f) 4.232×10^{-3}
g) 1.7×10^{18} h) 2.83×10^{-4}
i) 1×10^{-2}

Q15 7×10^6

Q16 6.38×10^8 cm

Q17 3.322×10^{-27} kg

Q18 a) 1.8922×10^{16} m
b) 4.7305×10^{15} m

Q19 a) 510000000 km^2
b) 3.62×10^8 km^2
c) 148000000 km^2

Pages 26-27 — Sets and Venn Diagrams

Q1 a) E = {prime numbers less than 12}
b) E = {2, 3, 5, 7, 11}

Answers: P26 — P32

Q2 **a)** L **b)** E.g. $1 \in K$ and $1.1 \notin K$

Q3 **a)** B = {–3, 1, 7, 8, 9, 12, 21}

b)

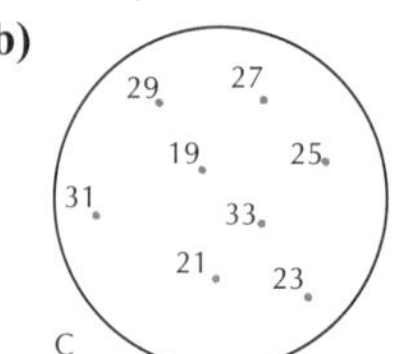

Q4 **a)**

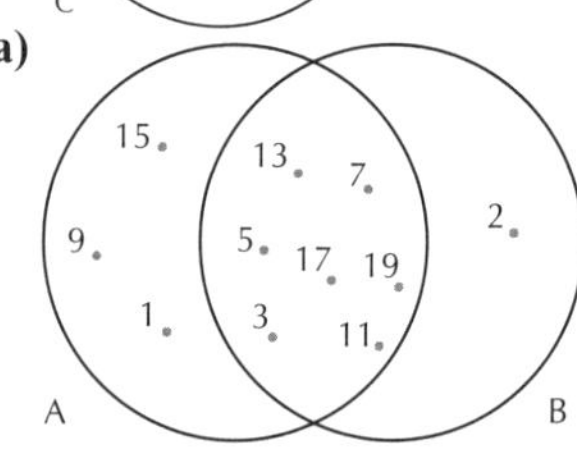

b)

Q5 **a)** 5
b) 2, 4, 7, 8
c) 8
d) 3, 5, 9

Q6 **a)** People who answered the survey
b) 9
c) $n(D \cup P) = 58$ and $n(D \cap P) = 3$

Q7 **a)** All the cows he counted
b) 19
c) $n(P) = 83$
d) $n(C \cup G) = 59$
e) $n(C') = 80$
f) $n(C \cap P) = 25$
g) $n(C \cap G \cap P) = 11$
h) $n(G \cap P \cap C') = 23$

Q8 **a)** false **g)** true
b) false **h)** false
c) true **i)** true
d) false **j)** false
e) false **k)** true
f) false **l)** false

Section Two — Algebra

Pages 28-30 — Powers and Roots

Q1 **a)** 16
b) 1000
c) 3 × 3 × 3 × 3 × 3 = 243
d) 4 × 4 × 4 × 4 × 4 × 4 = 4096
e) 1 × 1 × 1 × 1 × 1 × 1 × 1 × 1 × 1=1
f) 5 × 5 × 5 × 5 × 5 × 5 = 15 625

Q2 **a)** 2^8 (or 256)
b) 12^5 (or 248 832)
c) x^5 **d)** m^3
e) y^4 **f)** z^6

Q3 **b)** 10^7 **c)** 10^6
d) 10^8
e) Simply add the powers.

Q4 **b)** 2^3 **c)** 4^2
d) 8^3
e) Simply subtract the powers.

Q5 **a)** true **b)** true
c) false **d)** false
e) true **f)** false
g) false **h)** true
i) false **j)** true
k) true **l)** false

Q6 **a)** 3^{-3} **d)** 3^{-12}
b) 4^{25} **e)** 4^6
c) 10^{-13} **f)** 5^3

Q7 **a)** 275 **b)** 0.123
c) 53 400 **d)** 6.40×10^{-5}
e) 2.37 **f)** 2.31
g) 10.4 **h)** 0.843
i) 2.25 **j)** 2.18
k) 0.244 **l)** 0.965

Q8 **a)** 8.76 **b)** 4.17
c) 19.4 **d)** 219
e) 108 **f)** 91.9
g) 13.6 **h)** 17.8
i) 5.06

Q9 **a)** 0.008 **b)** 0.25
c) 1.53×10^{-5} **d)** 0.667
e) 2.24 **f)** 1.82
g) 1.55 **h)** 2.60
i) 0.512 **j)** 1.21
k) 0.0352 **l)** 7.28

Q10 **a)** 1.49 **b)** 20.1
c) 2.50 **d)** 6.55
e) 1.08 **f)** 8.78
g) 0.707 **h)** –0.380

Q11 **a)** 9.14 **b)** 1.50
c) 0.406 **d)** 476
e) 0.0146 **f)** 1.22
g) 84.5 **h)** 0.496
i) 165 **j)** 8.47

Q12 **a)** $k \times k$
b) $p \times p \times p \times q \times q$
c) $g \times t \times t$
d) $g \times g \times t \times t$
e) $-t \times -t$
f) $-(t \times t)$

Q13 **a)** a^3 **d)** c^3d^2
b) c^5 **e)** $4x^3$
c) a^2b^3 **f)** $6xy^3$

Q14 **a)** x^5 **m)** u^3
b) x **n)** 1
c) $-y^{13}$ **o)** gt
d) q^3 **p)** 1
e) b^9 **q)** k^{10}
f) $x^3 + x^2$ **r)** p^6
g) $-f^7$ **s)** v^2
h) x^7y^7 **t)** i
i) p^9q^6 **u)** g^7t^{14}
j) $-x$ **v)** x^{11}
k) 1 **w)** r^3
l) 1

Q15 **a)** $\frac{1}{k^2}$ **d)** y^2
b) $\frac{q^2}{p^3}$ **e)** a^4v^2
c) $\frac{g}{t^2}$ **f)** $\frac{a^4}{bv^2}$

Q16 **a)** $\frac{1}{h^6}$ **d)** $\frac{1}{v^2}$
b) $\frac{1}{g^3}$ **e)** $\frac{1}{w}$
c) $\frac{1}{t^4}$ **f)** $\frac{1}{a^4}$

Q17 **a)** $3a^3$ **f)** $\frac{1}{6j^2}$
b) p^4q^5 **g)** $\frac{b^{\frac{7}{10}}}{8}$
c) x^3y^4 **h)** $\frac{3}{u^{\frac{1}{2}}}$
d) x^2 **i)** $10d^{\frac{1}{8}}$
e) $2x^{\frac{1}{2}}$

Page 31 — Algebra Basics

Q1 **a)** –27°C **d)** +18°C
b) –22°C **e)** +15°C
c) +12°C **f)** –12°C

Q2 Expression **b)** is larger by 1.

Q3 **a)** $-4x$ **b)** $18y$

Q4 **a)** –1000, –10 **c)** 144, 16
b) –96, –6 **d)** 0, 0

Q5 –4

Q6 **a)** $-6xy$ **g)** $\frac{-5x}{y}$
b) $-16ab$ **h)** 3
c) $8x^2$ **i)** –4
d) $-16p^2$ **j)** –10
e) $\frac{10x}{y}$ **k)** $4x$
f) $\frac{-10x}{y}$ **l)** $-8y$

Q7 **a)** $15x^2 - x$
b) $13x^2 - 5x$
c) $-7x^2 + 12x + 12$
d) $30abc + 12ab + 4b$
e) $18pq + 8p$
f) $17ab - 17a + b$
g) $4pq - 5p - 9q$
h) $16x^2 - 4y^2$
i) $abc + 10ab - 11cd$
j) $-2x^2 + y^2 - z^2 + 6xy$

Q8 **a)** $x^2 + 4x + 3x + 12 = x^2 + 7x + 12$
b) $4x^2 + 6x + 6x + 9 = 4x^2 + 12x + 9$
c) $15x^2 + 3x + 10x + 2$
$= 15x^2 + 13x + 2$

Page 32 — Formulas from Words

Q1 **a)** $y = x + 5$ **d)** $y = x + 6^2$
b) $y = 7x + 4$ **e)** $y = x^2 \div 8$
c) $y = (x - 7) \div 3$ **f)** $y = x^2 \div 12$

Q2 **a)** $c = 25n$
b) $c = (25 + 1.25)n = 26.25n$

Q3 **a)** $N = n + 23$ **d)** $N = xn$
b) $N = n - 14$ **e)** $N = nx^2$
c) $N = 2n$

Q4 **a)** **i)** $4d$ cm **ii)** d^2 cm²
b) **i)** $a + b + c$ cm **ii)** $\frac{1}{2}cz$ cm²

Q5 $C = 10 + 5h$

Q6 $T = (73 + 27)p + 15l = 100p + 15l$

Q7 $S = (3 + \frac{1}{3}w)d$

Answers: P33 — P37

Page 33 — Multiplying Out Brackets

Q1 **a)** $4x + 4y - 4z$
b) $x^2 + 5x$
c) $-3x + 6$
d) $9a + 9b$
e) $-a + 4b$
f) $2x - 6$
g) $4e^2 - 2f^2 + 10ef$
h) $16m - 8n$
i) $6x^2 + 2x$
j) $-2ab + 11$
k) $-2x^2 - xz - 2yz$
l) $3x - 6y - 5$
m) $-3a - 4b$
n) $14pqr + 8pq + 35qr$
o) $x^3 + x^2$
p) $4x^3 + 8x^2 + 4x$
q) $8a^2b + 24ab + 8ab^2$
r) $7p^2q + 7pq^2 - 7q$
s) $16x - 8y$

Q2 **a)** $x^2 - 2x - 3$
b) $x^2 + 2x - 15$
c) $x^2 + 13x + 30$
d) $x^2 - 7x + 10$
e) $x^2 - 5x - 14$
f) $28 - 11x + x^2$
g) $6x - 2 + 9x^2 - 3x = 9x^2 + 3x - 2$
h) $6x^2 - 12x + 4x - 8 = 6x^2 - 8x - 8$
i) $4x^2 + x - 12x - 3 = 4x^2 - 11x - 3$
j) $4x^2 - 8xy + 2xy - 4y^2$
$= 4x^2 - 4y^2 - 6xy$
k) $12x^2 - 8xy + 24xy - 16y^2$
$= 12x^2 - 16y^2 + 16xy$
l) $9x^2 + 4y^2 + 12xy$

Q3 $15x^2 + 10x - 6x - 4 = 15x^2 + 4x - 4$

Q4 $4x^2 - 4x + 1$

Q5 **a)** $x^3 + x^2 - 4x - 4$
b) $x^3 + 10x^2 + 31x + 30$
c) $2x^3 - 15x^2 + 27x - 10$
d) $-x^3 - 4x^2 + 11x + 30$
e) $-2x^3 - 7x^2 - 2x + 3$
f) $6x^3 + 74x^2 + 144x + 40$
g) $-x^3 - 3x^2 + 9x + 27$
h) $4x^3 - 3x - 1$
i) $x^3 + 9x^2 + 27x + 27$

Q6 **a)** $(4x + 6)$ m
b) $(-3x^2 + 17x - 10)$ m^2

Q7 **a)** $(8x + 20)$ cm
b) $40x$ cm^2
c) $40x - 12x = 28x$ cm^2

Q8 **a)** Perimeter — $3x + 29$ cm
Area — $\frac{7x + 126}{2}$ cm^2
b) Perimeter — $(8x + 4)$ cm
Area — $(3x^2 + 14x - 24)$ cm^2
c) Perimeter — $(16x - 4)$ cm
Area — $(16x^2 - 8x + 1)$ cm^2
d) Perimeter — $(10x + 4)$ cm
Area — $(6x^2 - 5x - 6)$ cm^2

Page 34 — Factorising

Q1 **a)** $a^2(b + c)$
b) $a^2(5 + 13b)$
c) $a^2(2b + 3c)$
d) $a^2(a + y)$
e) $a^2(2x + 3y + 4z)$
f) $a^2(b^2 + ac^2)$

Q2 **a)** $x(x - 5)$
b) $2(x + 3)$
c) $3x(x + 4)$
d) $2x(2x - 3)$
e) $3xy(1 + 4x)$
f) $3(3x + 5)$
g) $5x(3xy - 5)$
h) $4pq(q - 5 + 2p)$
i) $2x(5x^3 + 3)$
j) $5x^2(3x - 4)$
k) $7x(3x + 2)$
l) $5xy(z + 4u)$

Q3 **a)** $4xyz(1 + 2) = 12xyz$
b) $4xyz\ (2 + 3) = 20xyz$
c) $8xyz(1 + 2x)$
d) $4xyz^2(5xy + 4)$

Q4 **a)** $(x + 3)(x - 3)$
b) $(y + 4)(y - 4)$
c) $(5 + z)(5 - z)$
d) $(6 + a)(6 - a)$
e) $(2x + 3)(2x - 3)$
f) $(3y + 2)(3y - 2)$
g) $(5 + 4z)(5 - 4z)$
h) $(1 + 6a)(1 - 6a)$
i) $(x^2 + 6)(x^2 - 6)$
j) $(x^2 + y^2)(x^2 - y^2)$
k) $(1 + ab)(1 - ab)$
l) $(10x + 12y)(10x - 12y)$

Q5 **a)** $(x + 2)(x - 2)$
b) $(12 + y^2)(12 - y^2)$
c) $(1 + 3xy)(1 - 3xy)$
d) $(7x^2y^2 + 1)(7x^2y^2 - 1)$

Q6 **a)** $16a^2b^2(4b - a)$
b) $q(p + r - pqr)$
c) $3(m^2 - 8)$
d) $b^2(b^2 - ab + c)$
e) $(a^2 - 13)(a^2 + 13)$
f) $3ab(3b - c)$
g) $(9 - z)(9 + z)$
h) $(6m - 5n)(6m + 5n)$
i) $mn(m + 3 - 2n^2)$
j) $(11p - 3q)(11p + 3q)$
k) $12(12x^2 - 9y^2 - 5z^2)$
l) $(8ab - 7cd)(8ab + 7cd)$

Page 35 — Manipulating Surds

Q1 **a)** $\sqrt{15}$ **b)** 2 **c)** x **d)** x **e)** 8 **f)** $\sqrt{5}$

Q2 3π cm^2

Q3 **a)** 1 **b)** $5\sqrt{3}$ **c)** $2\sqrt{2}$ **d)** $7 + 4\sqrt{3}$ **e)** $3\sqrt{5}$ **f)** $5\sqrt{2}$ **g)** $\sqrt{2}$ **h)** $3(\sqrt{2} - 1)$

Q4 **a)** $(1 + \sqrt{5})(1 - \sqrt{5}) = -4$, rational
b) $\frac{1 + \sqrt{5}}{1 - \sqrt{5}} = -\frac{1}{2}(3 + \sqrt{5})$, irrational

Q5 **a)** $(x + y)(x - y) = -1$, rational
b) $\frac{x + y}{x - y} = -3 - 2\sqrt{2}$, irrational

Q6 **a)** $\frac{\sqrt{2}}{2}$ **b)** $\frac{\sqrt{2}}{2}$ **c)** $\frac{\sqrt{10}a}{10}$ **d)** $\frac{\sqrt{xy}}{y}$ **e)** $\sqrt{2} - 1$ **f)** $3 - \sqrt{3}$ **g)** $\frac{2[\sqrt{6} - 1]}{5}$ **h)** $\frac{3 + \sqrt{5}}{2}$

Q7 $3\sqrt{3}$

Q8 $\sqrt{16} \times \sqrt{2} + 3\sqrt{2} = 7\sqrt{2}$

Q9 $19 + 6\sqrt{2}$

Pages 36-37 — Solving Equations

Q1 1

Q2 **a)** $x = \pm 3$ **b)** $x = \pm 6$ **c)** $x = \pm 3$ **d)** $x = \pm 3$ **e)** $x = \pm 1$

Q3 **a)** $x = 5$ **b)** $x = 4$ **c)** $x = 10$ **d)** $x = -6$ **e)** $x = 5$ **f)** $x = 9$

Q4 **a)** $x = 5$ **b)** $x = 2$ **c)** $x = 8$ **d)** $x = 17$ **e)** $x = 6$ **f)** $x = 5$ **g)** $x = \pm 2$

Q5 **a)** 15.5 cm **b)** 37.2 cm

Q6 £15.50

Q7 **a)** $x = 9$ **b)** $x = 2$ **c)** $x = 3$ **d)** $x = 3$ **e)** $x = 4$ **f)** $x = -1$ **g)** $x = 15$ **h)** $x = 110$ **i)** $x = \pm 6$ **j)** $x = 66$ **k)** $x = 700$ **l)** $x = 7\frac{1}{2}$

Q8 **a)** Joan — £x
Kate — £$2x$
Linda — £$(x - 232)$
b) $4x = 2632$
$x = 658$
c) Kate — £1316
Linda — £426

Q9 **a)** $2x + 32$ cm
b) $12x$ cm^2
c) $x = 3.2$

Q10 **a)** $x = 0.75$ **b)** $x = -1$ **c)** $x = -6$ **d)** $x = -1$ **e)** $x = 4$ **f)** $x = 13$

Q11 $x = 8$

Q12 $x = 1$

Q13 8 yrs

Q14 39, 35, 8

Q15 **a)** $y = 22$ **b)** $x = 8$ **c)** $z = -5$ **d)** $x = 19$ **e)** $x = 23$ **f)** $x = 7$ **g)** $x = \pm 3$ **h)** $x = \pm 4$ **i)** $x = \pm 7$

Q16 $x = 1\frac{1}{2}$

Q17 **a)** $x = 5$ **b)** $x = 9$

Answers: P37 — P43

Q18 $x = 1\frac{1}{2}$ AB = 5 cm
AC = 5½ cm
BC = 7½ cm

Pages 38-39 — Rearranging Formulas

Q1 **a)** $h = \frac{10 - g}{4}$ **b)** $c = 2d - 4$
c) $k = 3 + \frac{j}{2}$ **d)** $b = \frac{3a}{2}$
e) $g = \frac{8f}{3}$ **f)** $x = 2(y + 3)$
g) $t = 6(s - 10)$ **h)** $q = \pm\frac{\sqrt{p}}{2}$

Q2 **a)** $c = \frac{w - 500m}{50}$
b) 132

Q3 **a) i)** £38.00 **ii)** £48.00
b) $c = 28 + 0.25n$
c) $n = 4(c - 28)$
d) i) 24 miles **ii)** 88 miles
iii) 114 miles

Q4 **a)** $x = \pm\sqrt{y + 2}$
b) $x = y^2 - 3$
c) $s = \pm 2\sqrt{r}$
d) $g = 3f - 10$
e) $z = 5 - 2w$
f) $x = \pm\sqrt{\frac{3v}{h}}$
g) $a = \frac{v^2 - u^2}{2s}$
h) $u = \pm\sqrt{v^2 - 2as}$
i) $g = \frac{4\pi^2 l}{t^2}$

Q5 **a)** £Jx **b)** $P = T - Jx$
c) $J = \frac{T - P}{x}$ **d)** £16

Q6 **a) i)** £2.04 **ii)** £3.48
b) C = $(12x + 60)$ pence
c) $x = \frac{C - 60}{12}$
d) i) 36 **ii)** 48 **iii)** 96

Q7 **a)** $x = \frac{z}{y + 2}$
b) $x = \frac{b}{a - 3}$
c) $x = \frac{y}{4 - z}$
d) $x = \frac{3z + y}{y + 5}$
e) $x = \frac{-2}{y - z}$ or $\frac{2}{z - y}$
f) $x = \frac{2y + 3z}{2 - z}$
g) $x = \frac{-y - wz}{yz - 1}$ or $\frac{y + wz}{1 - yz}$
h) $x = \frac{-z}{4}$

Q8 **a)** $p = \frac{4r - 2q}{q - 3}$
b) $g = \frac{5 - 2e}{f + 2}$
c) $b = \frac{3c + 2a}{a - c}$
d) $q = \pm\sqrt{\frac{4}{p - r}} = \pm\frac{2}{\sqrt{p - r}}$
e) $a = \frac{2c + 4b}{4 + c - d}$
f) $x = \pm\sqrt{\frac{-3y}{2}}$
g) $k = \pm\sqrt{\frac{14}{h - 1}}$
h) $x = \left(\frac{4 - y}{2 - z}\right)^2$
i) $a = \frac{b^2}{3 + b}$
j) $m = -7n$
k) $e = \frac{d}{50}$
l) $y = \frac{x}{3x + 2}$

Q9 **a)** $y = \frac{x}{x - 1}$
b) $y = \frac{-3 - 2x}{x - 1}$ or $\frac{2x + 3}{1 - x}$
c) $y = \pm\sqrt{\frac{x + 1}{2x - 1}}$
d) $y = \pm\sqrt{\frac{1 + 2x}{3x - 2}}$

Page 40 — Factorising Quadratics

Q1 **a)** $(x + 5)(x - 2)$
$x = -5, x = 2$
b) $(x - 3)(x - 2)$
$x = 3, x = 2$
c) $(x - 1)^2$
$x = 1$
d) $(x - 3)(x - 1)$
$x = 3, x = 1$
e) $(x - 5)(x + 4)$
$x = 5, x = -4$
f) $(x + 1)(2x - 5)$
$x = -1, x = \frac{5}{2}$
g) $(3x + 7)(x - 1)$
$x = -\frac{7}{3}, x = 1$
h) $(x + 7)^2$
$x = -7$
i) $(x - 5)(2x + 3)$
$x = 5, x = -\frac{3}{2}$

Q2 **a)** $(x + 9)(x - 4)$
$x = -9, x = 4$
b) $x(x - 5)$
$x = 0, x = 5$
c) $(x - 7)(x + 3)$
$x = 7, x = -3$
d) $(x - 24)(x - 2)$
$x = 24, x = 2$
e) $(x + 7)(x - 2)$
$x = -7, x = 2$
f) $(x - 6)(x + 3)$
$x = 6, x = -3$

Q3 $x = \frac{1}{2}, x = -\frac{1}{2}$

Q4 **a)** $(x^2 - x)$ m^2
b) $x = 3$

Q5 **a)** $x(x + 1)$ cm^2
b) $x = 3$

Q6 **a)** x^2 m^2
b) $12x$ m^2
c) $x^2 + 12x - 64 = 0$
$x = 4$

Q7 **a)** area = $l(l - 0.75)$ cm^2
b) i) area = $(16l^2 - 12l)$ cm^2
ii) $16l^2 - 12l - 340 = 0 \Rightarrow l = 5$

Q8 **a)** $\frac{4}{x + 5}$ **b)** $\frac{x + 2}{x - 3}$
c) $\frac{2x + 3}{3x + 1}$

Pages 41-42 — The Quadratic Formula

Q1 **a)** 1.87, 0.13
b) 2.39, 0.28
c) 1.60, –3.60
d) 1.16, –3.16
e) 0.53, –4.53
f) –11.92, –15.08
g) –2.05, –4.62
h) 0.84, 0.03

Q2 **a)** –2, –6 **b)** 0.67, –0.5
c) 3, –2 **d)** 2, 1
e) 3, 0.75 **f)** 3, 0
g) 0.67 **h)** 0, –2.67
i) 4, –0.5 **j)** 4, –5
k) 1, –3 **l)** 5, –1.33
m) 1.5, –1 **n)** –2.5, 1
o) 0.5, 0.33 **p)** 1, –3
q) 2, –6 **r)** 2, –4

Q3 **a)** 0.30, –3.30 **b)** 3.65, –1.65
c) 0.62, –1.62 **d)** –0.55, –5.45
e) –0.44, –4.56 **f)** 1.62, –0.62
g) 0.67, –4.00 **h)** –0.59, –3.41
i) 7.12, –1.12 **j)** 13.16, 0.84
k) 1.19, –4.19 **l)** 1.61, 0.53
m) 0.44, –3.44 **n)** 2.78, 0.72

Q4 **a)** 1.7, –4.7 **b)** –0.27, –3.73
c) 1.88, –0.88 **d)** 0.12, –4.12
e) 4.83, –0.83 **f)** 1.62, –0.62
g) 1.12, –1.79 **h)** –0.21, –4.79
i) 2.69, –0.19 **j)** 2.78, 0.72
k) 1, 0 **l)** 1.5, 0.50

Q5 $x^2 - 3.6x + 3.24 = 0$
$x = 1.8$

Q6 **a)** $x^2 + 2.5x - 144.29 = 0$
$x = 10.83$
b) 48.3 cm

Page 43 — Completing the Square

Q1 **a)** $(x - 2)^2 - 9$
b) $(x - 1)^2$
c) $(x + \frac{1}{2})^2 + \frac{3}{4}$
d) $(x - 3)^2$
e) $(x - 3)^2 - 2$
f) $(x - 2)^2 - 4$
g) $(x + 1\frac{1}{2})^2 - 6\frac{1}{4}$
h) $(x - \frac{1}{2})^2 - 3\frac{1}{4}$
i) $(x - 5)^2$
j) $(x - 5)^2 - 25$
k) $(x + 4)^2 + 1$
l) $(x - 6)^2 - 1$

Q2 **a)** $x = 0.30, x = -3.30$
b) $x = 2.30, x = -1.30$
c) $x = 0.65, x = -4.65$
d) $x = 0.62, x = -1.62$
e) $x = 4.19, x = -1.19$

Answers: P43 — P47

f) $x = 2.82, x = 0.18$
g) $x = 1.46, x = -0.46$
h) $x = 2.15, x = -0.15$

Q3 **a)** $4 \pm \sqrt{29}$
b) $1 \pm \sqrt{6}$
c) $-3 \pm 2\sqrt{5}$
d) $-4 \pm 2\sqrt{3}$
e) $\frac{-3 \pm \sqrt{17}}{2}$
f) $\frac{-7 \pm \sqrt{37}}{2}$
g) $\frac{5 \pm 5\sqrt{5}}{2}$
h) $\frac{9 \pm 3\sqrt{5}}{2}$
i) $-1 \pm \frac{3\sqrt{2}}{2}$
j) $1 \pm \frac{2\sqrt{3}}{3}$
k) $\frac{7 \pm \sqrt{73}}{4}$
l) $\frac{5 \pm \sqrt{13}}{6}$

Q4 **a)** $(5, -28)$
b) $\left(\frac{7}{2}, -\frac{109}{4}\right)$
c) $(-2, -10)$
d) $\left(\frac{5}{8}, -\frac{41}{16}\right)$

Q5 **a)** $(-2, -5)$, minimum
b) $\left(\frac{11}{2}, \frac{97}{4}\right)$, maximum
c) $\left(-\frac{3}{2}, \frac{41}{4}\right)$, maximum
d) $(-2, -19)$, minimum
e) $\left(-\frac{5}{4}, -\frac{33}{8}\right)$, minimum
f) $(-1, 5)$, maximum

Q6 **a)**

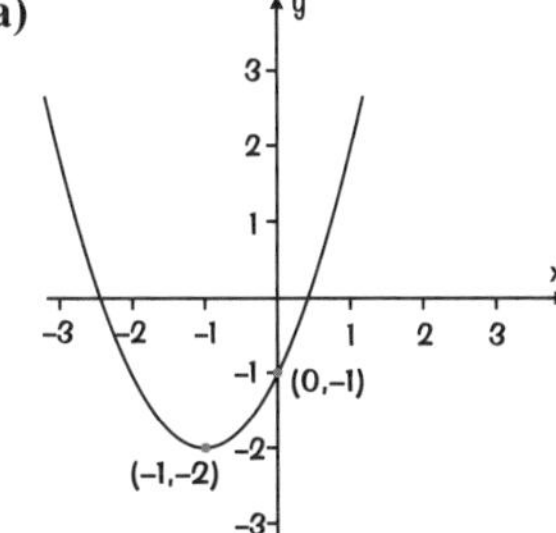

b)

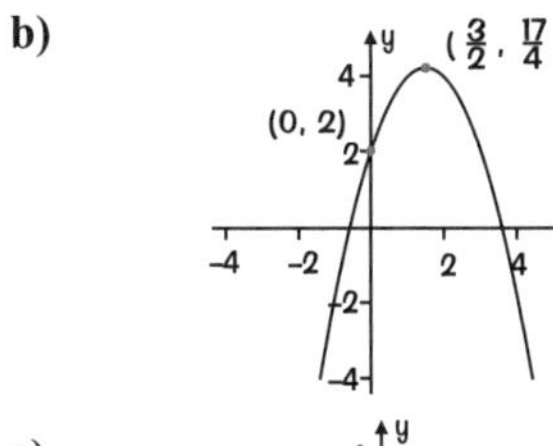

c)

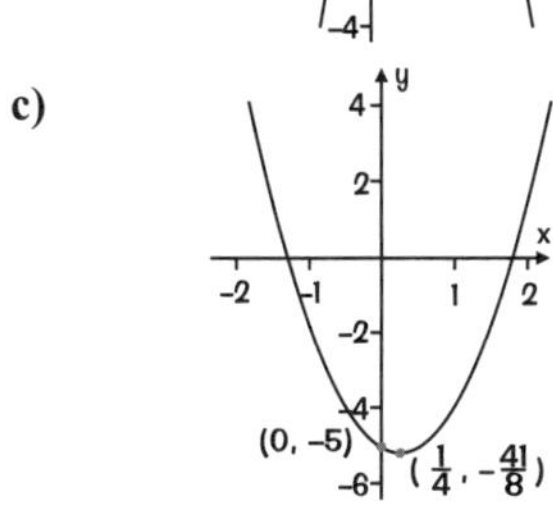

Q7 $y = \left(x + \frac{m}{2}\right)^2 - \frac{m^2}{4} + n$
This has its turning point when $x = -\frac{m}{2} = 1$. So $m = -2$.
When $x = 1$, $y = -\frac{m^2}{4} + n = -5$.
So $n = -4$.

Pages 44-45 — Algebraic Fractions

Q1 **a)** $\frac{3xy}{z}$ **b)** $\frac{12b^2}{c}$ **c)** $\frac{1}{3xy^2z^3}$ **d)** $\frac{q^3}{2r^3}$

Q2 **a)** $\frac{2}{xy}$ **b)** $\frac{3a^2b}{2}$ **c)** $\frac{y}{2x^2}$ **d)** $\frac{2qr^2}{3}$ **e)** $\frac{8x^2z^2}{y}$ **f)** $\frac{90ac^4}{b}$ **g)** $\frac{x^3}{5}$ **h)** $\frac{12a^3b^2}{5}$ **i)** $\frac{3a^4c^3}{2bd}$ **j)** 1 **k)** $\frac{3rt^2}{2}$ **l)** $\frac{d^6}{e^3f}$

Q3 **a)** $2x^2y$ **b)** a **c)** $\frac{3x^2}{y}$ **d)** $\frac{pq}{2}$ **e)** $2ef$ **f)** $5x^3$ **g)** $\frac{12yz}{x}$ **h)** $\frac{4a^3}{b}$ **i)** $\frac{5a^3}{b}$ **j)** $\frac{2x}{y^2z}$ **k)** $\frac{6}{n}$ **l)** $\frac{7g}{f}$

Q4 **a)** $\frac{3a-4}{2}$ **b)** $\frac{2x-y}{4}$ **c)** $\frac{5x+6}{3}$

Q5 **a)** $x = 5$
b) $x = 2$

Q6 **a)** $\frac{3+y}{2x}$ **b)** $\frac{1+y}{x}$ **c)** $\frac{2xy}{z}$ **d)** $\frac{6x+1}{3}$ **e)** $\frac{7x+6}{x}$ **f)** $\frac{14x+y}{6}$ **g)** $\frac{3x+2+y}{24}$ **h)** $\frac{x+2y-2}{10}$ **i)** $\frac{7x}{6}$ **j)** $\frac{37x}{42}$ **k)** $\frac{x(y+3)}{3y}$ **l)** $\frac{xyz+4x+4z}{4y}$

Q7 **a)** $\frac{4x-5y}{3}$ **b)** $\frac{4x-1}{y}$ **c)** $\frac{4x+3y-2}{2x}$ **d)** $\frac{2-2x}{x}$ **e)** $\frac{-1}{4x}$ **f)** $\frac{4x-y}{6}$ **g)** $\frac{z}{15}$ **h)** $\frac{m(12-n)}{3n}$ **i)** $\frac{b(14-a)}{7a}$ **j)** $\frac{-p+5q}{10}$ **k)** $\frac{-3p-4q}{4}$ **l)** $\frac{9x-4y+xy}{3y}$

Q8 **a)** $\frac{a^2}{b^2}$ **b)** 1 **c)** $\frac{3}{2r}$ **d)** $\frac{mn(pm+1)}{p^2}$ **e)** $\frac{2x}{x^2-y^2}$ **f)** $\frac{11}{6x}$ **g)** $\frac{2(a^2+b^2)}{a^2-b^2}$ **h)** $\frac{3}{4}$ **i)** $\frac{3x-6y}{8}$

Q9 **a)** $\frac{2(a^2+b^2)}{a^2-b^2}$ **b)** $\frac{8x^2+10x+11}{(2x-3)(2x+5)}$ **c)** $\frac{2x}{y}$ **d)** $\frac{5}{3(2x+1)}$ **e)** $\frac{1}{(x+4)(x-3)}$ **f)** $\frac{8(x+6)}{3}$

Pages 46-47 — Inequalities

Q1 **a)** $9 \le x < 13$ **b)** $-4 \le x < 1$
c) $x \ge -4$ **d)** $x < 5$
e) $x > 25$ **f)** $-1 < x \le 3$
g) $0 < x \le 5$ **h)** $x < -2$

Q2
a) 4 5 6 7 8 9 10
b) –2 –1 0 1 2 3 4
c) –6 –5 –4 –3 –2 –1 0 1 2 3
d) –3 –2 –1 0 1 2 3 4
e) –3 –2 –1 0 1 2 3 4
f) 4 5 6 7 8 9 10
g) –4 –3 –2 –1 0 1 2
h) –4 –3 –2 –1 0 1 2

Q3 **a)** $x > 3$ **b)** $x < 4$
c) $x \le 5$ **d)** $x \le 6$
e) $x \ge 7.5$ **f)** $x < 4$
g) $x < 7$ **h)** $x < 4$
i) $x \ge 3$ **j)** $x > 11$
k) $x < 3$ **l)** $x \ge -½$
m) $x \le -2$ **n)** $x > 5$
o) $x < 15$ **p)** $x \ge -2$

Q4 Largest integer for x is 2.

Q5 $\frac{11-x}{2} < 5, x > 1$

Q6 **a)** $1 < x < 8$ **f)** $-1 < x < 23$
b) $0 \le x \le 8$ **g)** $-2 \le x < 4$
c) $2 < x < 4$ **h)** $-51 < x \le -11$
d) $-4 \le x < -1$ **i)** $-16 < x \le 5$
e) $5 \le x \le 10$

Q7 $1130 \le 32x$
36 classrooms are needed.

Q8 50 guests (including bride and groom), $900 \ge 18x$

Q9 $x \ge 2, \quad y > 1, \quad x + y \le 5$

Answers: P47 — P51

Q10

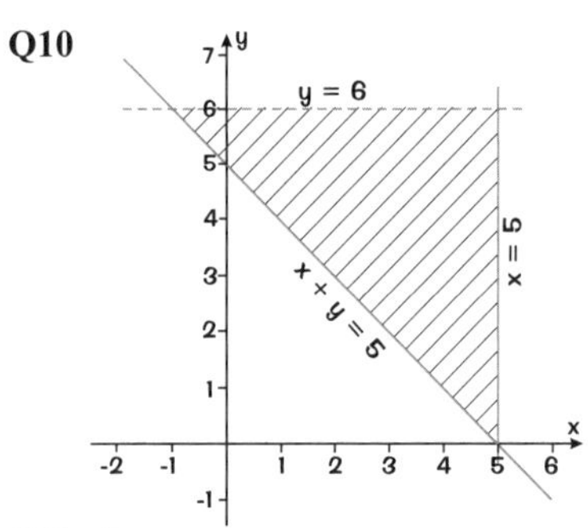

Q11 **a)** –5 –4 –3 –2 –1 0 1 2 3 4 5

b) –5 –4 –3 –2 –1 0 1 2 3 4 5

c) –5 –4 –3 –2 –1 0 1 2 3 4 5

d) –5 –4 –3 –2 –1 0 1 2 3 4 5

e) –5 –4 –3 –2 –1 0 1 2 3 4 5

f) –5 –4 –3 –2 –1 0 1 2 3 4 5

g) –5 –4 –3 –2 –1 0 1 2 3 4 5

h) –5 –4 –3 –2 –1 0 1 2 3 4 5

Q12 **a)** $x > 5$, $y \geq 7$, $x + y \geq 14$

b)

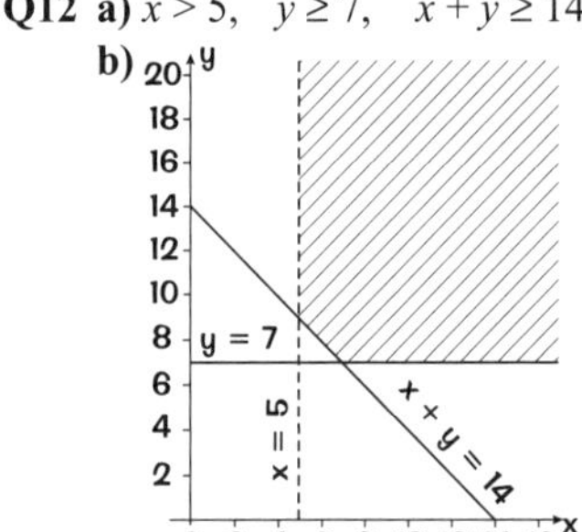

Q13 **a)** $-2 < x < 3$

b) $-5 \leq x \leq -1$

c) $x < -2$ or $x > -1$

d) $x \leq 2$ or $x \geq 8$

e) $x < -2$ or $x > 9$

f) $-7 < x < -5$

g) $x \leq 4$ or $x \geq 5$

h) $-3 < x < 1$

i) $-2 \leq x \leq -\frac{3}{2}$

j) $x < \frac{1}{2}$ or $x > 4$

k) $-\frac{2}{3} < x < 1$

l) $x \leq -4$ or $x \geq \frac{5}{4}$

Page 48 — Simultaneous Equations and Graphs

Q1 **a)** $x = 3, y = 3$ **b)** $x = 2, y = 5$
c) $x = 1, y = 2$ **d)** $x = 1, y = 2$
e) $x = 1, y = 4$ **f)** $x = 1, y = 2$
g) $x = 2, y = 3$ **h)** $x = 2, y = 3$
i) $x = 5, y = 2$ **j)** $x = 3, y = 4$

Q2 **a)** $x = 0, x = 1$
b) $x = 2.7, x = -0.7$
c) $x = 3.4, x = -2.4$
d) $x = 1.6, x = -2.6$
e) $x = 0.7$
f) $x = 3.4, x = -2.4$
g) $x = 1.6, x = -2.6$

Q3

x	-4	-3	-2	-1	0	1	2	3	4
$-\frac{1}{2}x^2$	-8	-4.5	-2	-0.5	0	-0.5	-2	-4.5	-8
+5	5	5	5	5	5	5	5	5	5
y	-3	0.5	3	4.5	5	4.5	3	0.5	-3

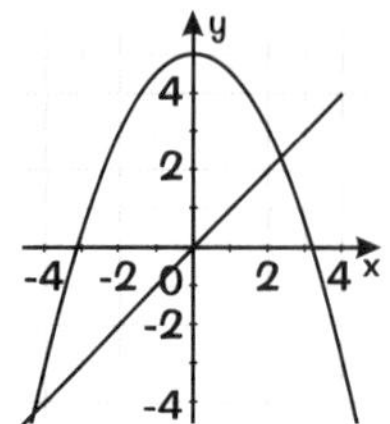

a) $x = 3.2, x = -3.2$
b) $x = 4, x = -4$
c) $x = 2.3, x = -4.3$

Page 49 — Simultaneous Equations

Q1 **a)** $x = 4, y = 18$ OR $x = -3, y = 11$
b) $x = 6, y = 28$ OR $x = -3, y = 1$
c) $x = 1.5, y = 4.5$ OR $x = -1, y = 2$
d) $x = -3, y = 33/5$ OR $x = 2, y = \frac{28}{5}$
e) $x = -\frac{1}{4}, y = \frac{17}{4}$ OR $x = -3, y = 40$
f) $x = -\frac{2}{3}, y = \frac{31}{3}$ OR $x = -4, y = 57$

Q2 **a)** $x = 1, y = 2$
b) $x = 0, y = 3$
c) $x = -1\frac{1}{2}, y = 4$
d) $x = 5, y = 23$ OR $x = -2, y = 2$
e) $x = \frac{1}{3}, y = -\frac{29}{3}$ OR $x = 4, y = 38$
f) $x = \frac{1}{2}, y = -\frac{3}{2}$ OR $x = -2, y = 6$
g) $x = 1, y = 9$
h) $x = 8, y = -\frac{1}{2}$
i) $x = -1, y = 3$

Q3 **a)** $6x + 5y = 430$
$4x + 10y = 500$
b) $x = 45, y = 32$

Q4 7 chickens
4 cats

Q5 5 g (jellies are 4 g)

Q6 $3y + 2x = 18$
$y + 3x = 6$ $x = 0, y = 6$
$4y + 5x = 7$
$2x - 3y = 12$ $x = 3, y = -2$
$4x - 6y = 13$
$x + y = 2$ $x = 2\frac{1}{2}, y = -\frac{1}{2}$

Q7 $5m + 2c = 344$
$4m + 3c = 397$
$m = 34$p, $c = 87$p

Q8 $x = 12, y = 2$

Page 50 — Sequences

Q1 **a)** 10, 12, 14; even numbers
b) 9, 11, 13; odd numbers
c) 25, 36, 49; square numbers
d) 125, 216, 343; cube numbers

Q2 **a)** 31, 36, 41 **b)** 5
c) $5n + 1$ **d)** 101

Q3 **a)** 10, 12, 14, $2n$
b) 9, 11, 13, $2n - 1$
c) 25, 30, 35, $5n$
d) 17, 20, 23, $3n + 2$
e) 19, 22, 25, $3n + 4$
f) 32, 37, 42, $5n + 7$
g) 46, 56, 66, $10n - 4$
h) 82, 89, 96, $7n + 47$

Q4 **a)** $4n - 3$
b) 75 is not in the sequence because when the expression is set to equal 75, n is not a whole number.

Q5 24, 35, 48

Q6 **a)** $16\frac{7}{8}, 16\frac{9}{16}, 16\frac{23}{32}, 16\frac{41}{64}$
b) The 10th term will be the mean of the 8th and 9th terms.

Q7 592

Q8 **a)** $d = 2, a = -1$
b) 9800

Page 51 — Proof

Q1 $(2n + 1)^2 - (2n - 1)^2 - 10$
$= (4n^2 + 4n + 1) - (4n^2 - 4n + 1) - 10$
$= 8n - 10$
Dividing this by 8 gives $n - \frac{5}{4}$ (not a whole number), so the expression is not a multiple of 8.

Q2 $n + (n + 1) + (n + 2)$
$= 3n + 3 = 3(n + 1)$
Dividing this by 3 gives n + 1 (a whole number), so the sum is divisible by 3.

Q3 $2a \times 2b = 4ab = 2 \times 2ab$. This is divisible by 2 and so is even.

Q4 $2n + (2n + 2) + (2n + 4)$
$= 6n + 6 = 6(n + 1)$
Dividing this by 6 gives n + 1 (a whole number), so the sum is a multiple of 6.

Q5 **a)** E.g. 3 and 1 are both odd numbers but if you add them together you get 4, which is even so the statement is wrong.
b) E.g. If n = 6, $n^2 = 36$, which is divisible by 4, but 6 is not divisible by 4, so the statement is wrong.

Q6 E.g. If a = 1 and b = –1, then $a^2 = 1$ and $b^2 = 1$. So $a^2 = b^2$ but a does not equal b, so the statement is wrong.

Q7 $5^{20} - 5^{19}$
$= 5 \times 5^{19} - 5^{19}$
$= 5^{19}(5 - 1) = 4 \times 5^{19}$
$= 2 \times 2 \times 5^{19}$
$= 2n$ where $n = 2 \times 5^{19}$
So $5^{20} - 5^{19}$ is even.

Q8 $3^8 - 1$ can be factorised to $(3^4 - 1)(3^4 + 1)$, so it has factors that are not equal to itself or 1. Therefore, it is not a prime number.

Q9 $\frac{y^2 + 1}{y^2} - \frac{x^2 + 1}{x^2} = \frac{x^2 - y^2}{(xy)^2}$
$x^2 - y^2 < 0$ since $x > 0$, $y > 0$ and $x < y$.
Also, $(xy)^2$ is always positive.
Therefore, $\frac{x^2 - y^2}{(xy)^2} < 0$
which means $\frac{y^2 + 1}{y^2} - \frac{x^2 + 1}{x^2} < 0$

Answers: P51 — P56

Q10 $n^2 - 2n + 2 + (n + 1)^2 - 2(n + 1) + 2$
$= n^2 - 2n + 2 + n^2 + 2n + 1 - 2n - 2 + 2$
$= 2n^2 - 2n + 3$
$= 2n^2 - 2n + 2 + 1$
$= 2(n^2 - n + 1) + 1$
$= 2x + 1$ where $x = (n^2 - n + 1)$
So the sum of two consecutive terms is an odd number.

Q11 If $x^2 + 3 > 2x + 1$,
then $x^2 - 2x + 2 > 0$
and $(x - 1)^2 + 1 > 0$
This is always true as $(x - 1)^2$ cannot be negative. So the inequality always holds and Fay is correct.

Page 52 — Direct and Inverse Proportion

Q1 $y = 20$
Q2 $y = 184.8$
Q3 $y = 2$
Q4 $x = 2$
Q5

x	1	2	3	4	5	6
y	48	24	16	12	9.6	8

Q6

x	1	2	5	10
y	100	25	4	1

x	2	4	6	8
y	24	6	$2^2/_3$	1.5

Q7 4 kg
Q8 **a)** $r = 96$ **b)** $s = 4$
c) $r = 600$ **d)** $s = -8$
Q9 9.5 N kg^{-1}

Section Three — Graphs, Functions and Calculus

Pages 53-54 — Coordinates

Q1

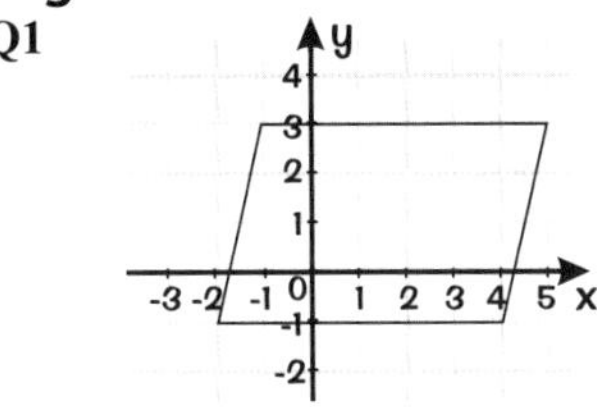

missing coordinate = (5, 3)

Q2

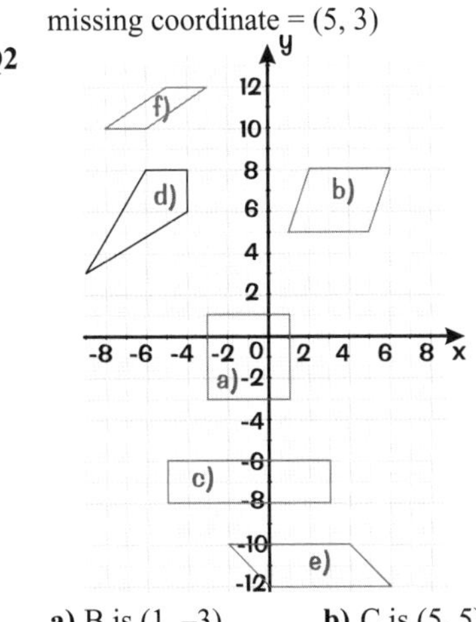

a) B is (1, –3) **b)** C is (5, 5)
c) A is (–5, –8) **d)** D is (–4, 6)
e) D is (0, –12) **f)** C is (–3, 12)

Q3

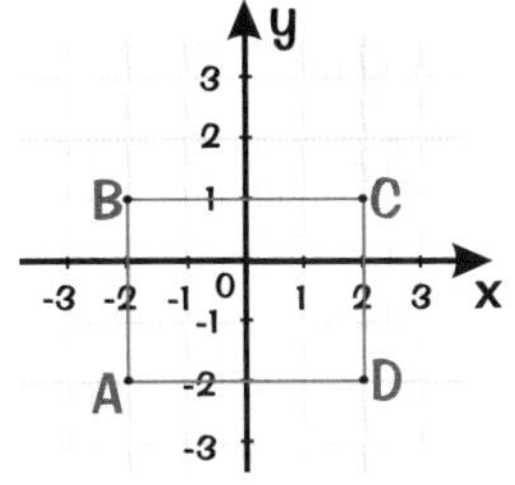

C = (2, 1), D = (2, –2)

Q4 (-2, 7)

Q5

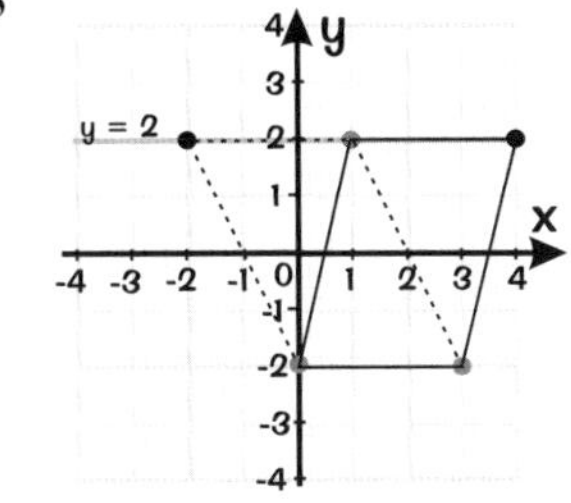

Possible coordinates = (–2, 2) and (4, 2).

Q6 **a)** (3,4) **b)** (5.5,5)
c) (5.5,11) **d)** (8.5,9)
e) (3,3.5) **f)** (9.5,9.5)
g) (20,41.5) **h)** (30.5,20.5)

Q7 (110, 135)

Q8 **a)** (2,5.5) **b)** (0.5,1.5)
c) (2,–2.5) **d)** (1,–1)
e) (2,3) **f)** (4,–0.5)
g) (–13,–12.5) **h)** (–5,–7)

Pages 55-56 — Straight-Line Graphs

Q1 **a)** B **f)** F
b) A **g)** C
c) F **h)** B
d) G **i)** D
e) E **j)** H

Q2

x	-4	-3	-2	-1	0	1	2	3	4
3x	-12	-9	-6	-3	0	3	6	9	12
-1	-1	-1	-1	-1	-1	-1	-1	-1	-1
y	-13	-10	-7	-4	-1	2	5	8	11

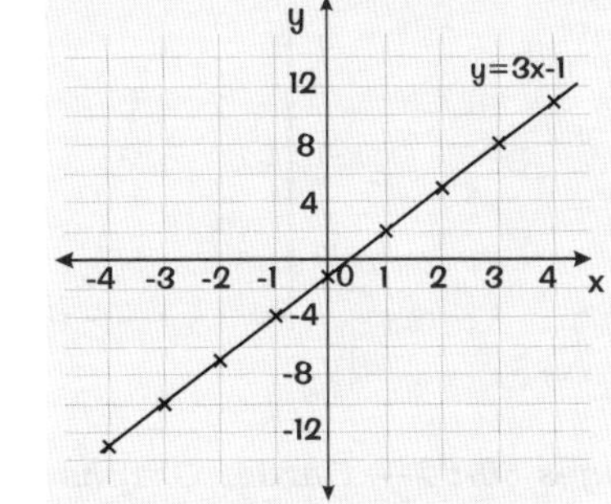

Q3

x	-6	-4	-2	0	2	4	6
1/2 x	-3	-2	-1	0	1	2	3
-3	-3	-3	-3	-3	-3	-3	-3
y	-6	-5	-4	-3	-2	-1	0

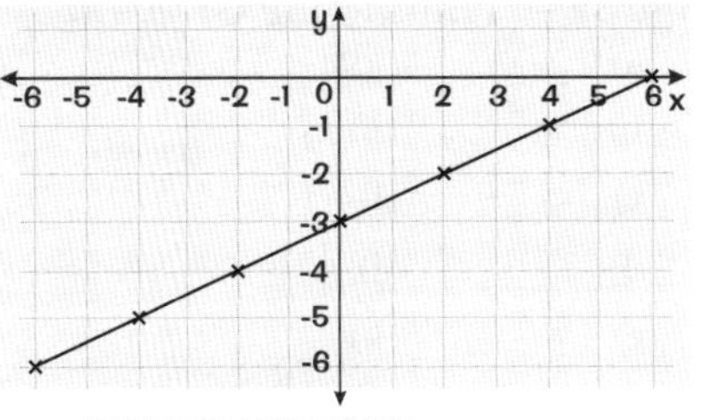

Q4

x	0	3	8
y	3	9	19

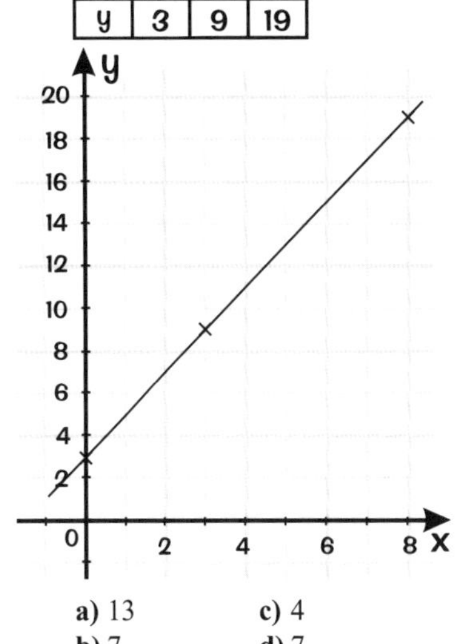

a) 13 **c)** 4
b) 7 **d)** 7

Q5

x	-8	-4	8
y	-5	-4	-1

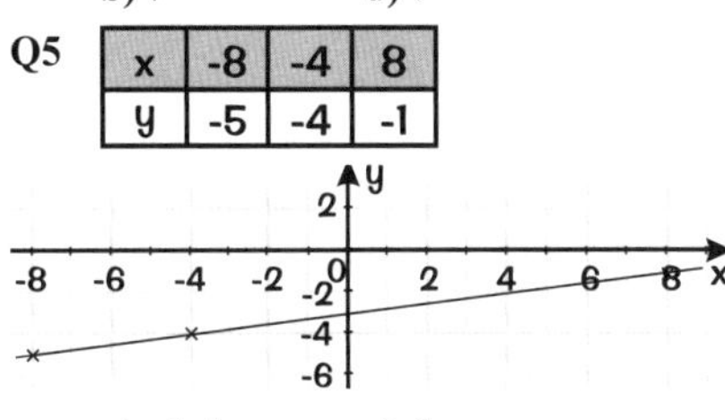

a) –2.5 **c)** 4
b) –3 **d)** 6

Q6

Number of Units used	0	100	200	300
Cost using method A	10	35	60	85
Cost using method B	40	45	50	55

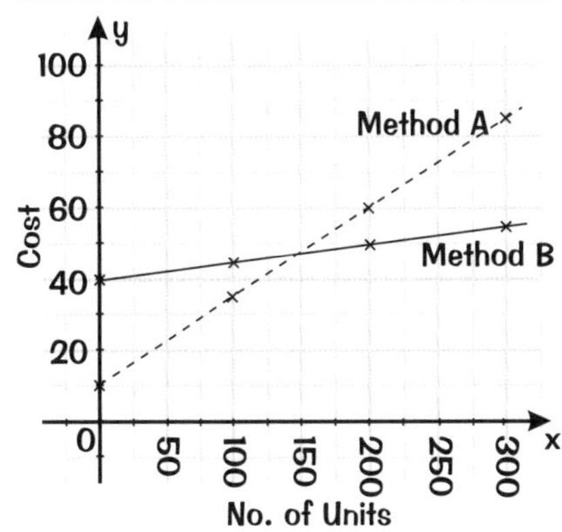

a) i) £27.50 **ii)** £43.50
b) Method A
c) 150 units

Answers: P57 — P62

Page 57 — Finding the Gradient

Q1 **a)** $-\frac{1}{2}$ **g)** 4
b) 3 **h)** 1
c) $-\frac{1}{4}$ **i)** -1
d) -2 **j)** $\frac{1}{3}$
e) $-\frac{2}{3}$ **k)** $-\frac{1}{2}$
f) $-\frac{8}{3}$ **l)** 3

Q2 **a)** 2 **d)** -2
b) $\frac{1}{2}$ **e)** $\frac{1}{2}$
c) -1 **f)** $-\frac{3}{4}$

Q3 **a)** A and C
b) (1, 2)

Q4 The gradient is –0.23 so it's a red run.

Page 58 — "y = mx + c"

Q1 **a)** $m = 4$, (0, 3)
b) $m = 3$, (0, –2)
c) $m = 2$, (0, 1)
d) $m = -3$, (0, 3)
e) $m = 5$, (0, 0)
f) $m = -2$, (0, 3)
g) $m = -6$, (0, –4)
h) $m = 1$, (0, 0)
i) $m = -\frac{1}{2}$, (0, 3)
j) $m = \frac{1}{4}$, (0, 2)
k) $m = \frac{4}{3}$, (0, 2)

Q2 **a)** $y = \frac{7}{2}x - 1$ **d)** $y = \frac{1}{4}x - 3$
b) $y = \frac{1}{2}x + 4$ **e)** $y = -\frac{1}{2}x$
c) $y = -\frac{1}{5}x + 7$ **f)** $y = -2x - 6$

Q3 **a)** $y = x + 4$ **c)** $y = -x$
b) $y = 3x + 2$ **d)** $y = -3x + 4$

Q4 **a)** $y = x$ **c)** $y = -3x + 3$
b) $y = 3x$ **d)** $y = -2x - 4$

Q5 **a)** $x = 4$ **c)** $y = 7$
b) $x = 8$ **d)** $y = 9$

Q6 (7, 20) and (5, 14)

Q7 **a)** $m = 3$
b) $y = 3x + 1$

Q8 **a)** $m = -2$
b) $y = -2x - 3$

Page 59 — Quadratic Graphs

Q1

x	–4	–3	–2	–1	0	1	2	3	4
$y=2x^2$	32	18	8	2	0	2	8	18	32

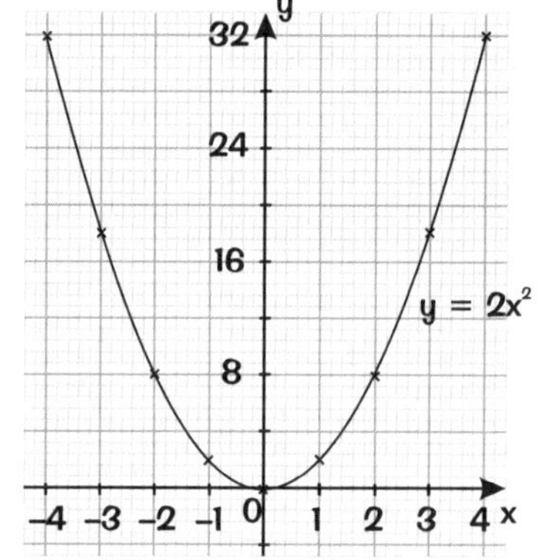

Q2

x	–4	–3	–2	–1	0	1	2	3	4
x^2	16	9	4	1	0	1	4	9	16
$y=x^2+x$	12	6	2	0	0	2	6	12	20

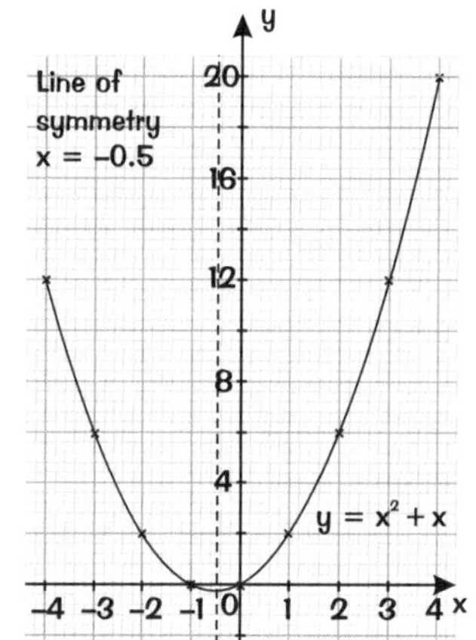

Q3 **a)**

x	–4	–3	–2	–1	0	1	2	3	4
3	3	3	3	3	3	3	3	3	3
$-x^2$	–16	–9	–4	–1	0	–1	–4	–9	–16
$y=3-x^2$	–13	–6	–1	2	3	2	–1	–6	–13

b)

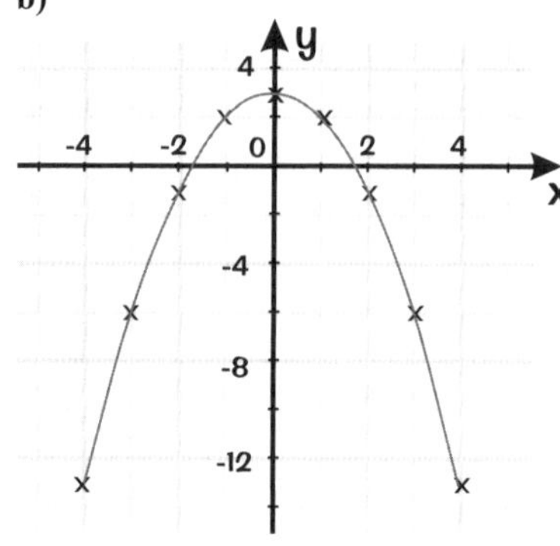

c) 3

Pages 60-64 — Harder Graphs

Q1 **a)** Reciprocal **f)** Reciprocal
b) Reciprocal **g)** Straight line
c) Reciprocal **h)** Cubic
d) Quadratic **i)** Cubic
e) Quadratic **j)** Cubic

Q2 **a)** ix **g)** viii
b) iv **h)** vi
c) iii **i)** x
d) vii **j)** v
e) xi **k)** ii
f) xii **l)** i

Q3

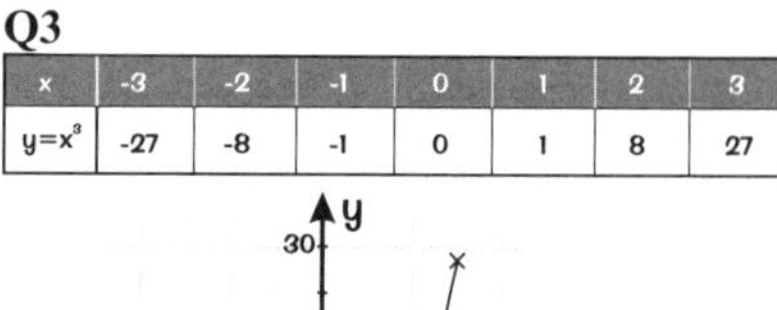

x	-3	-2	-1	0	1	2	3
$y=x^3$	-27	-8	-1	0	1	8	27

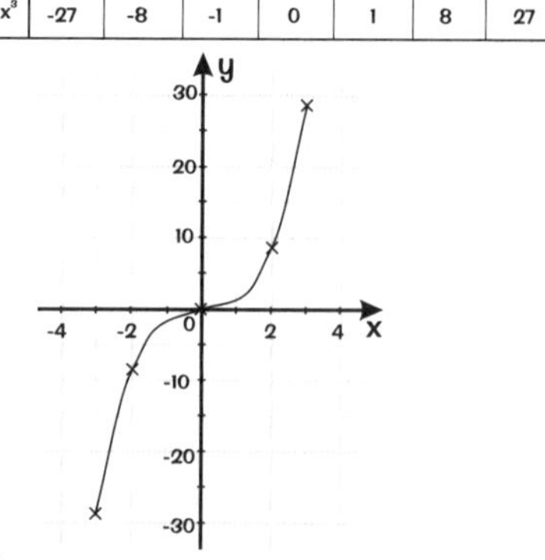

Q4

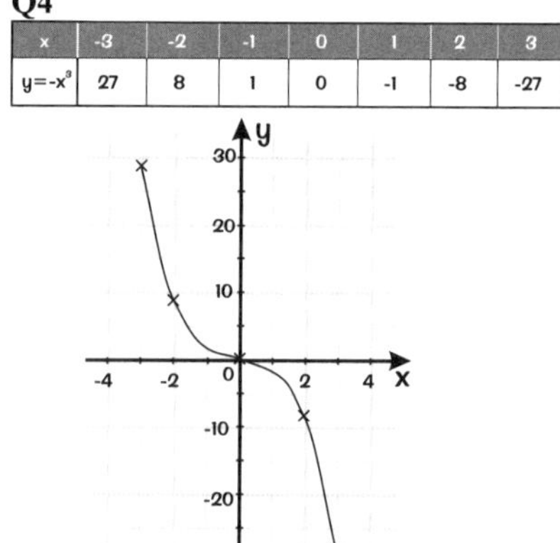

x	-3	-2	-1	0	1	2	3
$y=-x^3$	27	8	1	0	-1	-8	-27

Q5

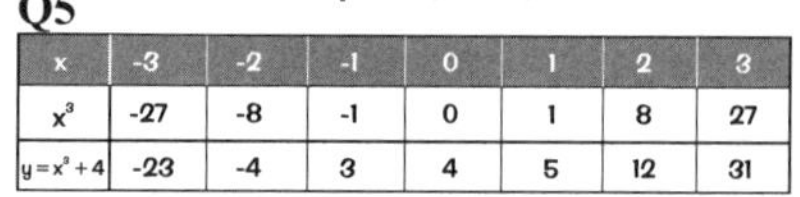

x	-3	-2	-1	0	1	2	3
x^3	-27	-8	-1	0	1	8	27
$y=x^3+4$	-23	-4	3	4	5	12	31

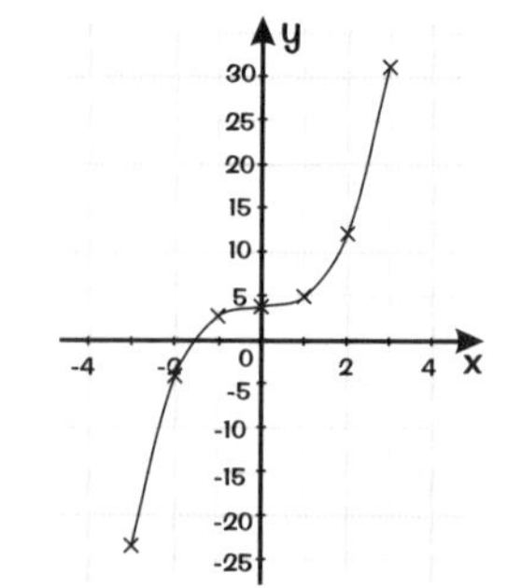

Q6

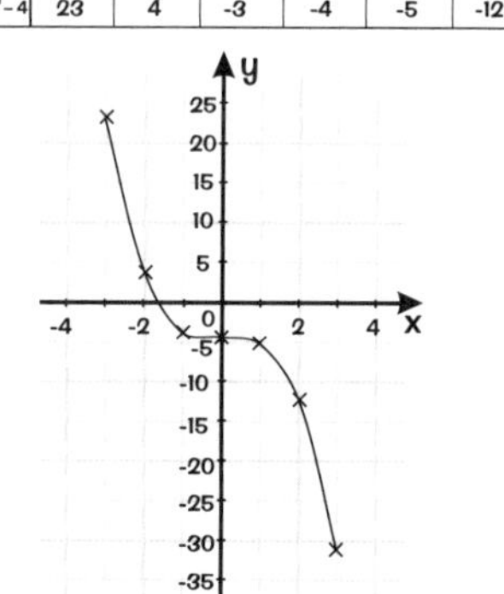

x	-3	-2	-1	0	1	2	3
$-x^3$	27	8	1	0	-1	-8	-27
$y=-x^3-4$	23	4	-3	-4	-5	-12	-31

Answers: P63 — P66

Q7

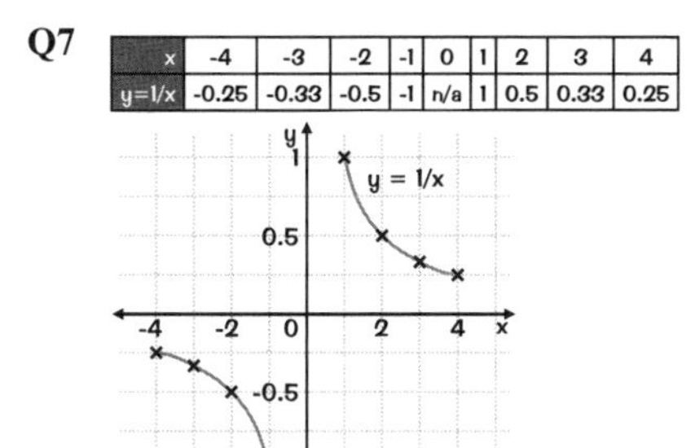

x	-4	-3	-2	-1	0	1	2	3	4
y=1/x	-0.25	-0.33	-0.5	-1	n/a	1	0.5	0.33	0.25

Q8

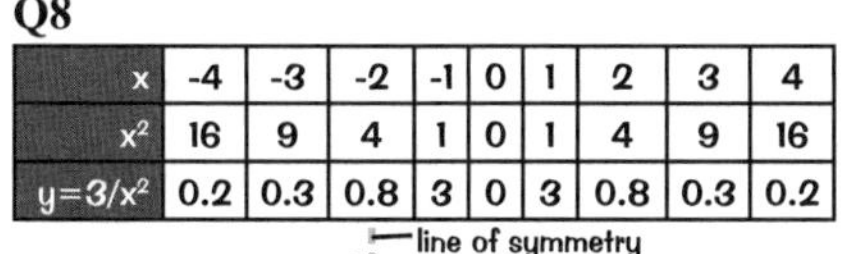

x	-4	-3	-2	-1	0	1	2	3	4
x²	16	9	4	1	0	1	4	9	16
y=3/x²	0.2	0.3	0.8	3	0	3	0.8	0.3	0.2

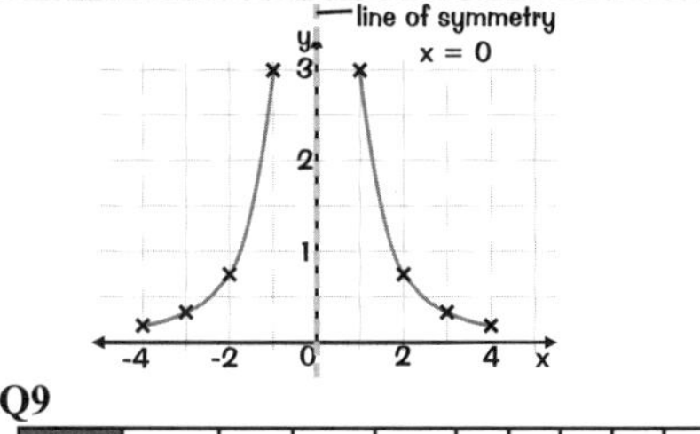

Q9

x	-4	-3	-2	-1	0	1	2	3	4
y=2ˣ	0.06	0.1	0.3	0.5	1	2	4	8	16

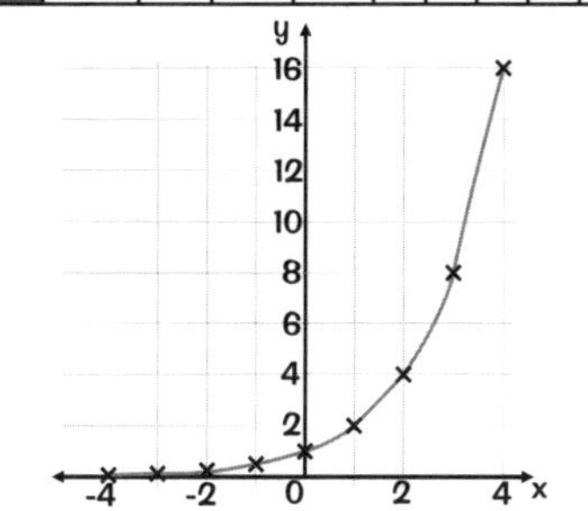

c) Anything to the power of 0 is 1.

Q10

x	-3	-2	-1	0	1	2	3
3ˣ	0.04	0.1	0.3	1	3	9	27
6/x	-2	-3	-6	n/a	6	3	2
y=3ˣ – 6/x	2.04	3.1	6.03		-3	6	25

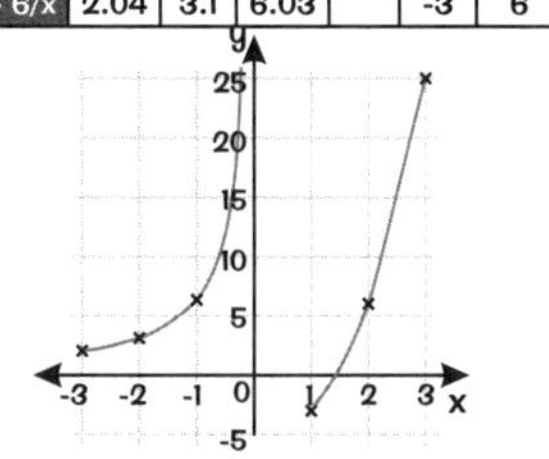

Q11 **a)** B **b)** E **c)** D

Q12

x	0°	30°	60°	90°	120°	150°	180°
sin x	0	0.5	0.87	1	0.87	0.5	0
cos x	1	0.87	0.5	0	-0.5	-0.87	-1
tan x	0	0.58	1.73	—	-1.73	-0.58	0

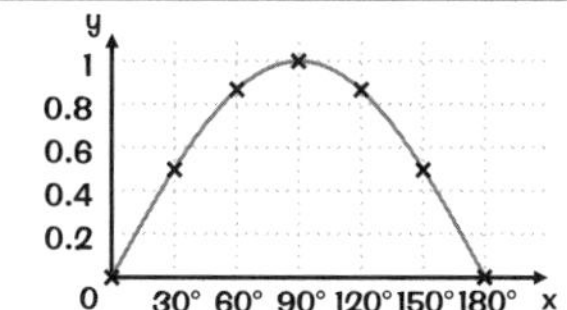

Q13

x	360°	405°	450°	495°	540°
cos x	1	0.71	0	-0.71	-1

x	585°	630°	675°	720°
cos x	-0.71	0	0.71	1

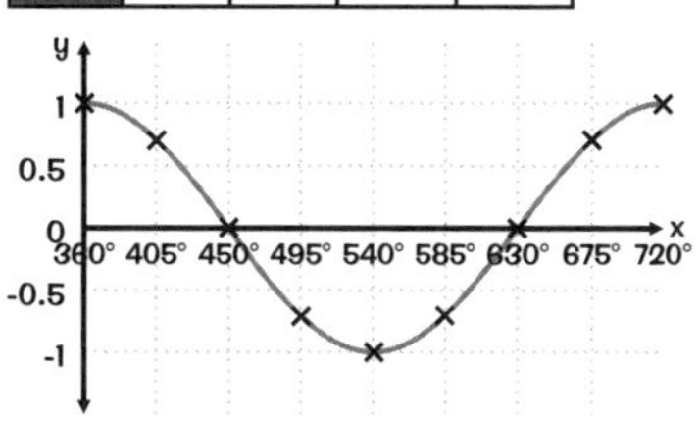

Page 65 — Functions

Q1 **a)** $f(x) = 3 + x$
b) $f(x) = 790 - 41x$
c) $f(x) = 3(9x^2 + 2)$

Q2 **a)** $x = 4.5$ **b)** $x = \pm 1$ **c)** $x = \pm 0.31$ **d)** $x = \pm 2$ **e)** $x = 0.27$ or -7.27 **f)** $x = 5$

Q3 **a)** $x > 4$ **b)** $x \leq 0$ **c)** $x = 0$ **d)** $x < -3.5$ **e)** $x = -0.75$

Q4 **a)** $f(8) = 44$
b) $g(3) = -6$
c) $f(-4) = -4$
d) $gf(x) = 3 - (4x + 12)^2$
e) $fg(x) = 4(3 - x^2) + 12$
f) $gf(2) = -397$

Q5 **a)** $h^{-1}(x) = x - 6$
b) $f^{-1}(x) = \frac{11}{x} - 1$
c) $g^{-1}(h(x)) = \frac{4}{3}(6 + x)$
d) $f^{-1}(g(x)) = \frac{44}{3x} - 1$
e) $h^{-1}(f(5)) = -4\frac{1}{6}$
f) $h^{-1}(g(-1)) = -6.75$

Q6 **a)** $f(-1) = -\frac{2}{3}$ **b)** $g(9) = 554$ **c)** $kj(-3) = 210$ **d)** $n^{-1}(2) = -14.5$ **e)** 12 **f)** 0.75

Q7 **a)** $hi(x) = (11 \div (-x + \frac{x^2}{2})) - 8$
b) $m^{-1}(x) = \frac{10(x-3)+4}{18} = \frac{5x-9}{9}$
c) $p^{-1}(q(x)) = \frac{\left(\frac{13}{x-2}\right) - 5}{8} = \frac{23-5x}{8x-16}$

Pages 66-67 — Graph Transformations

Q1 **a)** to **d)**

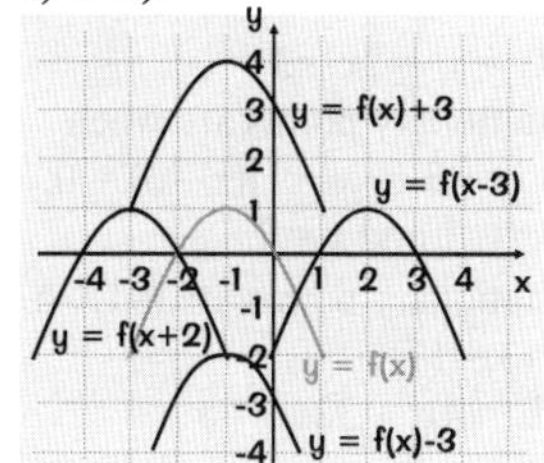

e) and **f)**

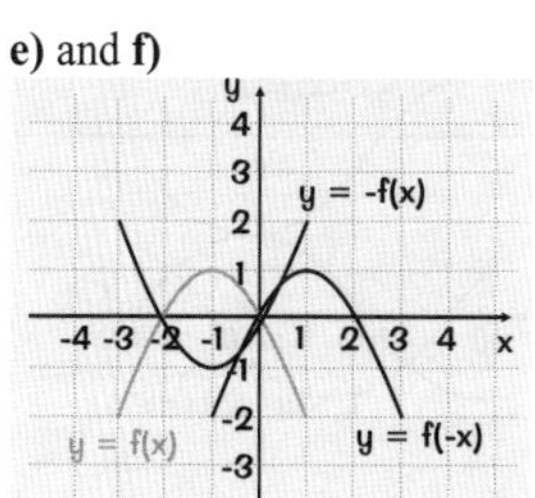

g) to **i)**

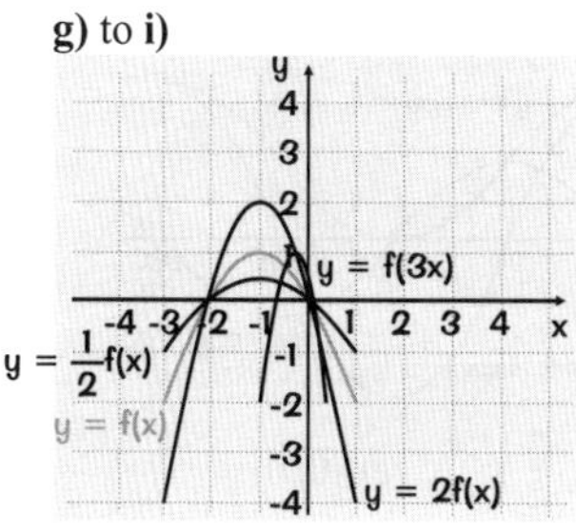

Q2 **a)** to **d)**

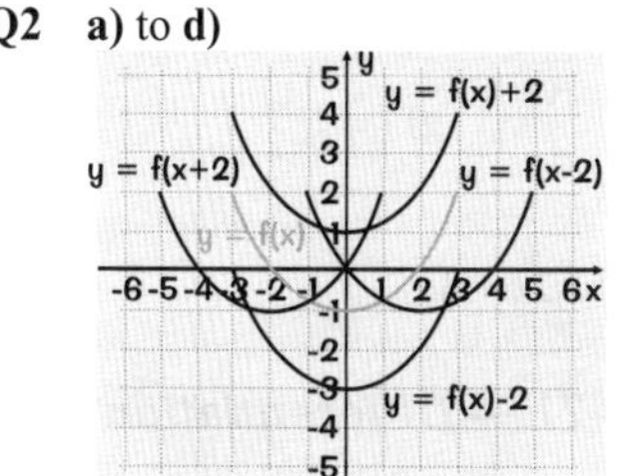

e) and **f)**

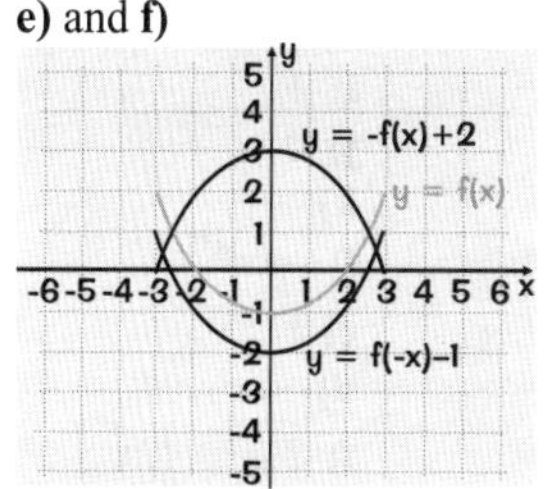

g) and **h)**

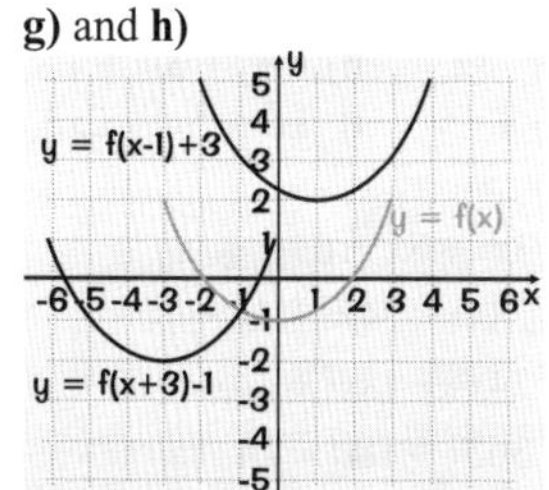

i) and **j)**

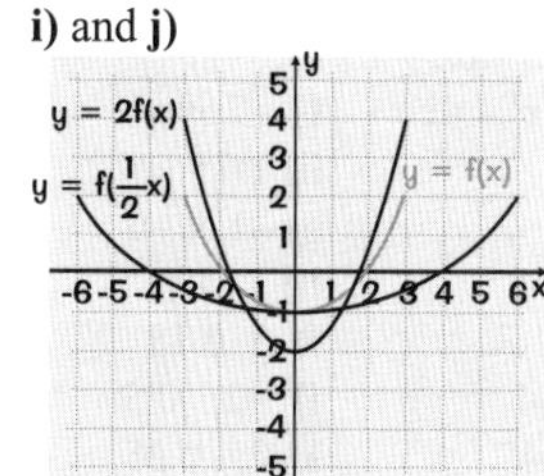

Q3 Graph is reflected in the x-axis and the y-axis.

Answers: P67 — P74

Q4 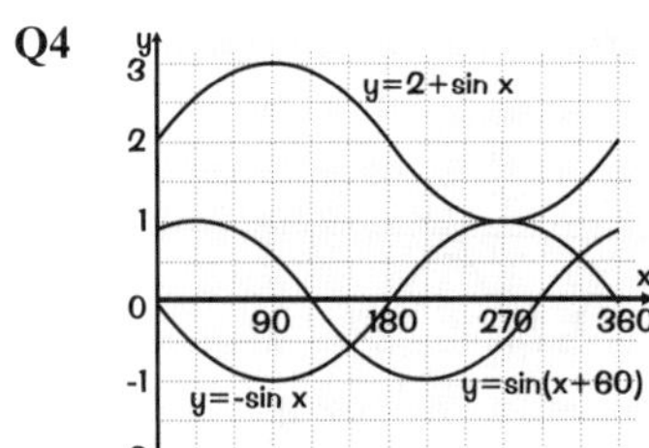

Q5 a) to **c)**

Q6 a) $(4, \frac{3}{2})$ **e)** $(0, 0)$
b) $(1, \frac{7}{2})$ **f)** $(-1, \frac{3}{2})$
c) $(1, -\frac{3}{2})$ **g)** $(\frac{4}{3}, \frac{11}{2})$
d) $(1, 3)$

Q7 $y = -x^3 - 2x + 4$

Pages 68–71 — Differentiation

Q1 a) $4x^3$ **b)** $2x$ **c)** $13x^{12}$ **d)** $4x$ **e)** $15x^2$ **f)** $28x^3$ **g)** $2x^3$ **h)** 33 **i)** 1 **j)** 0 **k)** $-9x^2$ **l)** $-4x^{15}$

Q2 a) $7a^6$ **b)** $50t^4$ **c)** 1 **d)** $-4w^5$

Q3 a) $5x^4$ **b)** $14x^6$ **c)** 1 **d)** $4x + 1$ **e)** $9x^8 + 3$ **f)** $21x^2 + 12x$ **g)** $32x^7 + 2x$ **h)** $15x^4 + 3x^2 + 1$ **i)** $3x^8 + 5x^4 + 2x$

Q4 $36x^3 + 3x^2 + 8x + 6$

Q5 $15x^4 + 28x^3 + 24x^2 + 4x + 10$

Q6 $40x^7 + 24x^5 + 48x^3 + 14x$

Q7 $44d^3 + 36d^2 + 18d + 14$

Q8 a) $-12x^2 - 2x$ **b)** $15x^2 + 6x + 1$ **c)** $-18x^2 - 4x$ **d)** $6x^2 + 2x - 8$ **e)** $-1/x^2$ **f)** $-2/x^3$

Q9 i) 1 **ii)** 1.75

Q10 a) –2, –2 **b)** 5, 44 **c)** –2, 4 **d)** 2, –4 **e)** –2, 4 **f)** 6, 24 **g)** –1.5, –6 **h)** 3, 12 **i)** 3, 0.75 **j)** –2, –0.5 **k)** 2, –0.25 **l)** –2, 0.25

Q11 $dy/dx = 3x^2 + 6x + 1$. Gradient at $x = 2$ is $3(2^2) + (6\times2) + 1 = 12 + 12 + 1 = 25$. This is positive, so must be Graph B as Graphs A and C have negative gradients at $x = 2$.

Q12 (2, 14)

Q13 (0.5, 8)

Q14 a) Between 23 minutes and 2 hours 37 minutes = 2 hours 14 minutes.
b) $v = -2t + 3$
c) after 30 mins, $v = 2$ km/h, after 1 hour, $v = 1$ km/h

Q15 a) $d = 2t^2(t + 1) = 2(6)^2(6 + 1) = 2 \times 36 \times 7 = 504$ metres
b) Velocity = $d(d)/dt = 6t^2 + 4t$
So after 6 seconds: Velocity = $6(6)^2 + 4(6) = 216 + 24 = 240$ m/s
c) Acceleration = d(velocity)/dt = $12t + 4$. So after 6 seconds acceleration = $12(6) + 4 = 76$ m/s^2

Q16 a) $v = 4(40)^2 + 2(40) + 3$
$v = 6483$ m/s
b) Acceleration = $dv/dt = 8t + 2$, so acceleration after 40 s is: $8(40) + 2 = 322$ m/s^2

Q17 a) $dy/dx = 4x$, so turning point is when $4x = 0$, so $x = 0$.
Turning point is (0, 0).
Graph is $y = ax^2$ graph, $a > 0$, so turning point is a minimum.
b) $dy/dx = 10x + 1$, so turning point is when $10x + 1 = 0$, so $x = -0.1$.
Turning point is (–0.1, –0.05).
Graph is $y = ax^2$ graph, $a > 0$, so turning point is a minimum.
c) $dy/dx = 6x + 2$, so turning point is when $6x + 2 = 0$, so $x = -1/3$.
Turning point is $(-1/3, -5\frac{1}{3})$.
Graph is $y = ax^2$ graph, $a > 0$, so turning point is a minimum.
d) $dy/dx = -2x + 4$, so turning point is when $-2x + 4 = 0$, so $x = 2$.
Turning point is (2, –4).
Graph is $y = ax^2$ graph, $a < 0$, so turning point is a maximum.
e) $y = x^2 - 4x - 32$, so $dy/dx = 2x - 4$
Turning point is when $2x - 4 = 0$, so $x = 2$.
So turning point is (2, –36).
Graph is $y = ax^2$ graph, $a > 0$, so turning point is a minimum.

Q18 a) $4x^3 - 2x - 3$
b) $20x^4 + 36x^3$
c) $2x^2 + \frac{2}{x^3} + 10$
d) $3x^2 + 15x - \frac{12}{x^5}$

Q19 a) $dy/dx = x^2 - 2x - 3$
So stationary points are when $x^2 - 2x - 3 = (x + 1)(x - 3) = 0$.
So $x = -1$ and $x = 3$.
So stationary points are $(-1, -6\frac{1}{3})$ and (3, –17).
b) $dy/dx = 4x^2 - 32x + 48$
So stationary points are when $x^2 - 8x + 12 = (x - 2)(x - 6) = 0$.
So $x = 2$ and $x = 6$.
So stationary points are $(2, 42\frac{2}{3})$ and (6, 0).
c) $dy/dx = 2x^2 - 9x - 5$
So stationary points are when $2x^2 - 9x - 5 = (2x + 1)(x - 5) = 0$.
So $x = -0.5$ and $x = 5$.
So stationary points are $(-0.5, -\frac{17}{24})$ and $(5, -56\frac{1}{6})$.
d) $dy/dx = 3x^2 + 12x + 12$
So stationary points are when $x^2 + 4x + 4 = (x + 2)(x + 2) = 0$.
So $x = -2$.
So stationary point is (–2, –7).

Q20 a) $C = -20(0)^3 + 40(0)^2 - 10 = -10$ °C.
b) $dC/dt = -60t^2 + 80t$
So $dC/dt = -60(0.5)^2 + 80(0.5) = 25$ °C.
c) $dC/dt = 0$, so $-60t^2 + 80t = 0$,
Using the quadratic formula:
$$t = \frac{-b \pm \sqrt{b^2 - 4ac}}{2a}$$
$$t = \frac{-80 \pm \sqrt{80^2 - 4(-60)(0)}}{2(-60)}$$
so $t = 0$ and $1\frac{1}{3}$
The heater was switched off after 1 hour 20 minutes.

Section Four — Geometry and Measure

Page 72 — Scale Drawings

Q1 10 cm long and 7.5 cm wide

Q2 65 cm long and 17 cm wide

Q3 13 mm wide gap, 78 cm wide oven.

Q4 a) Room 4 cm long and 3 cm wide
b) Window 2 cm, door 0.75 cm

Q5 a) 3.3 cm **b)** 13.2 km **c)** 42.8 km

Q6 a) 12.25 m **b)** 4.04 m^2

Pages 73-74 — Geometry

Q1 a) $x = 47°$ **b)** $y = 154°$ **c)** $z = 22°$ **d)** $p = 35°$, $q = 45°$

Q2 a) $a = 146°$
b) $m = 131°$, $z = 48°$
c) $x = 68°$, $p = 112°$
d) $s = 20°$, $t = 90°$

Q3 a) $a = 130°$
b) $b = 56°$
c) $c = 48°$

Q4 a) $x = 96°$, $p = 38°$
b) $a = 108°$, $b = 23°$, $c = 95°$
c) $d = 120°$, $e = 60°$, $f = 60°$, $g = 120°$
d) $h = 155°$, $i = 77.5°$, $j = 102.5°$, $k = 77.5°$

Q5 a) $b = 70°$ $c = 30°$ $d = 50°$ $e = 60°$ $f = 150°$
b) $g = 21°$ $h = 71°$ $i = 80°$ $j = 38°$ $k = 92°$
c) $l = 35°$ $m = 145°$ $n = 55°$ $p = 125°$

Answers: P74 — P79

Q6 **a)** $x = 162°$ $y = 18°$
b) $x = 87°$ $y = 93°$
$z = 93°$
c) $a = 30°$ $2a = 60°$
$5a = 150°$ $4a = 120°$

Q7 **a)** $a = 141°$, $b = 141°$, $c = 39°$,
$d = 141°$, $e = 39°$
b) $a = 47°$, $b = 47°$, $c = 133°$,
$d = 43°$ $e = 43°$
c) $m = 140°$, $n = 140°$, $p = 134°$,
$q = 46°$, $r = 40°$

Pages 75-76 — Polygons

Q1 Isosceles.

Q2

order of rotational symmetry = 6.

Q3 **a)** Angles at a point sum to 360°, hence m + m + r = 360°.
Angles in a pentagon sum to 540°. We know two angles are 90°, so we are left with 360°. The only angles left are m, m and r so m + m + r must equal 360°.
b) r°.
c)

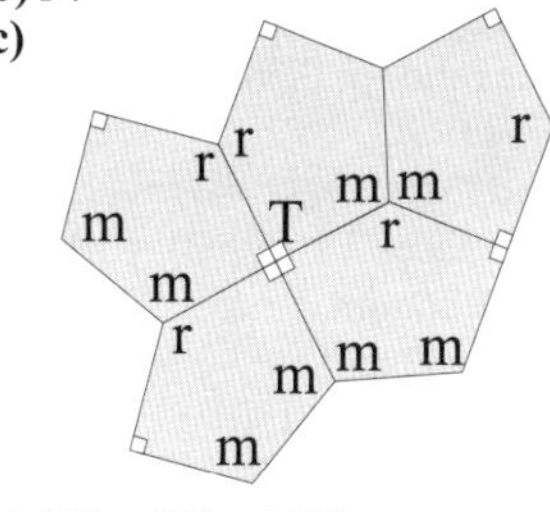

Q4 **a)** 90° + 60° = 150°

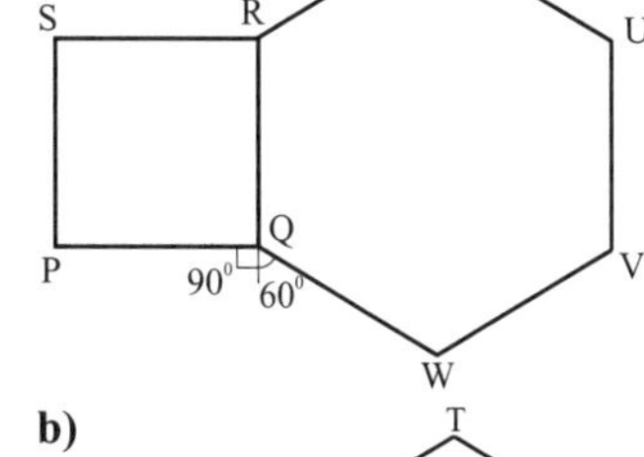

b)

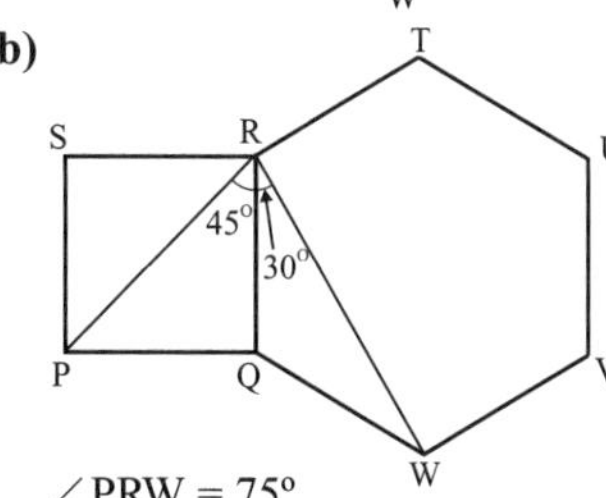

∠PRW = 75°

c) 180 – (360/n) = 150
180n – 360 = 150n
30n = 360 ⇒ n = 12

Q5 540° – (100° + 104° + 120°)
= 216° for two equal angles
∴1 angle = 108°

Q6 **a)** Interior angle = 165°
b) Exterior angle = 180° – 165° = 15°
Sum of exterior angles = 15 × 24
= 360°

Q7 **a)** $\frac{360}{5} = 72°$
b) $\frac{180-72}{2} = 54°$
c) i) 90° **ii)** 36°
d) Lines ST and BE are parallel, so angle ABE = angle BAS = 36° (alternate angles).
Triangle ABE is isosceles, so angle BEA = angle ABE = 36°.

Q8 (2n – 4)90 = 2520, n = 16

Q9 **a)** $(\frac{360}{5}) \div 2 = 36°$
b) OX = 5 cos 36° = 4.045 cm.
Hence MX = 5 – 4.045 = 0.95 cm.

Q10 a)

D E C F B G A H

b) Angle CDE = angle DEF
$= \frac{(2\times 8-4)90}{8} = 135$
so angle EFC = $\frac{360-2(135)}{2} = 45°$
OR exterior angle = 45° = angle EFC (alternate angles).

Page 77 — Symmetry

Q1 a) b) c)

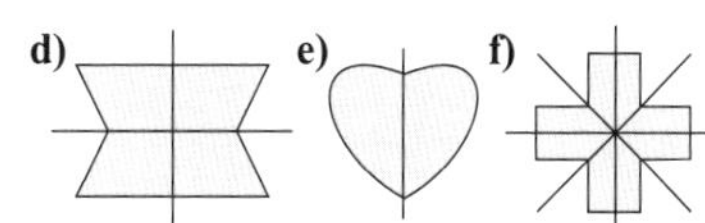

Q2 **a)** 6 **b)** 8 **c)** 5 **d)** 3

Q3

1 2 1
Order of Rotation
1 1 2 2

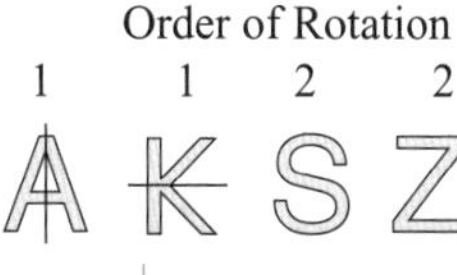

Q4 **a)** Order of Rotation = 3

b) Order of Rotation = 1

c)

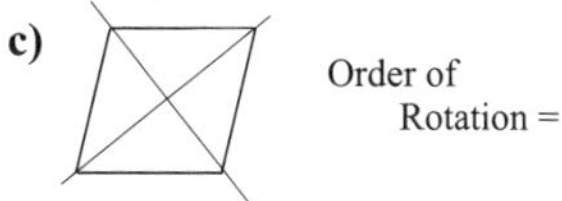

Order of Rotation = 2

d) Order of Rotation = 1

e)

Order of Rotation = 8

f) Order of Rotation = 2

Pages 78-80 — Circle Geometry

Q1 BD bisects AC and meets it at an angle of 90°, so BD must be a diameter of the circle.
So BD = 2 × 9 = 18 m

Q2 **a)** BD = 5 cm (as the tangents BD and CD are equal).
b) Angle COD = 70° (= 180° – (20° + 90°)), since the tangent CD meets the radius OC at an angle of 90°.
c) Angle COB = 140° (since angle BOD equals angle COD).

Q3 Both 90°

Q4 **a)** BAD = 80° (opposite angle C in cyclic quadrilateral)
b) EAB = 180 – 80 – 30 = 70°

Q5 **a)** BOE = 106° (angle at centre)
b) ACE = 32° (angle in opposite segment)

Q6 **a)** ACD = 70° (angle in opposite segment)
b) BAD = 180 – (30 + 70) = 80° (opposite angles of a cyclic quadrilateral total 180°)

Q7 **a)** Angles in the same segment.
b) $3x + 40 = 6x - 50$
$90 = 3x$
$30 = x$
angle ABD = 3(30) + 40 = 130°

Q8 There are 2 ways of answering this question.

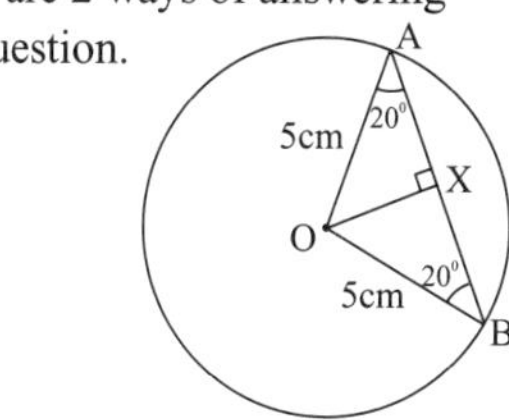

A diameter through O bisects the chord at X so cos 20° = $\frac{AX}{5}$ ⇒
AX = 4.698 and
AB = 9.40 cm.
or by the sine rule $\frac{AB}{\sin 140°} = \frac{5}{\sin 20°}$
AB = $\frac{5\sin 140°}{\sin 20°}$ = 9.40 cm

Q9 **a)** Angle ACB is an angle in a semicircle, so it is a right angle.
So area of ABC = ½ × AC × BC
= ½AC² = 64 cm²
By Pythagoras,
AB² = AC² + BC² = 2AC²
= 4(½AC²)
= 4 × 64 = 256
So AB = $\sqrt{256}$ = 16 cm
b) BX = 3AX and
BX + AX = 16 cm, so BX = 12 cm and AX = 4 cm
AB and DE are intersecting chords, so AX × BX = DX × EX
12 × 4 = 6 × EX
EX = 48 ÷ 6 = 8 cm
So DE = 8 + 6 = 14 cm

Answers: P79 — P85

Q10 **a)** Angle ABD = 70° (angle at centre = 2 × angle at circumference)
b) Angle ABC = 90° (angle in semicircle)
c) Angle DBC = 20° (90° – 70°)

Q11 **a)** 90° (angle in a semicircle)
b) The angle at A = 90° (tangent and radius are perpendicular).
The third angle in the triangle is 180 – 90 – 23 = 67° and so $x = 90 - 67 = 23°$.
Or, by opposite segment theorem: x = angle ABC = 23°.

Q12 **a)** With AD as a chord, angle ABD = ACD = 30° (same segment); angle AXB = 85° (vertically opposite angles).
The third angles must be the same in both triangles so the triangles must be similar.
b) Ratio of lengths = $\frac{4}{8} = \frac{1}{2}$
so XB = 7.25 cm
c) angle BDC = 180 – 85 – 30 = 65°

Q13 **a)** 90° (angle in a semicircle)
b) Pythagoras is needed here:
$AC^2 + 3^2 = 10^2$
$AC^2 = 100 - 9 = 91$
AC = 9.54 cm
c) AD = 5 cm so DC = 9.54 – 5 = 4.54 cm then Pythagoras gives
$(4.54)^2 + 3^2 = (DOB)^2$
$20.606 + 9 = (DOB)^2$
So DOB = 5.44 cm

Q14 **a)** Both angles are 90° (angle in a semicircle)
b) 3 × 6.5 = 5 × BX
So BX = 3.9 cm
c) 2.5 × (2.5 + 3 + 6.5) = 6 × YF
So YF = 5 cm

Pages 81-82 — The Four Transformations

Q1 **a), b), c)** — see diagram.

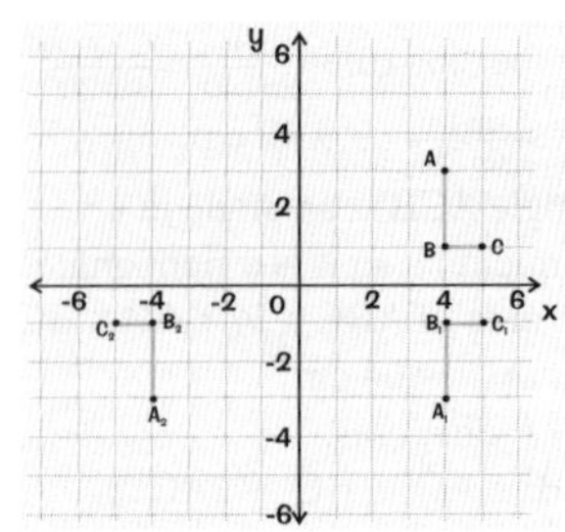

d) Rotation of +180° (or –180) about (0, 0)

Q2 **a), b), d), e)** — see diagram

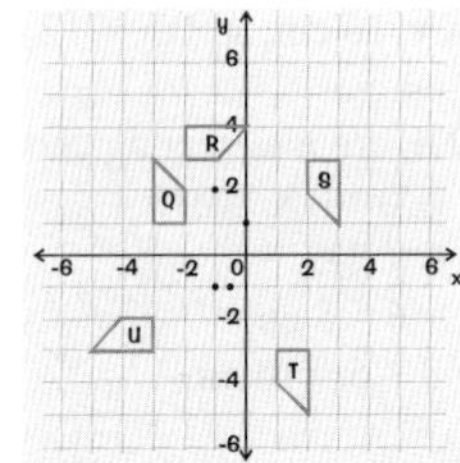

c) Rotation of +180° (or –180) about (0, 2).
f) 90° rotation anticlockwise about $\left(-\frac{1}{2}, -\frac{1}{2}\right)$.

Q3 **a)**

b) $\overrightarrow{QO} = \begin{pmatrix}-3\\-4\end{pmatrix}$
$T = \begin{pmatrix}11\\8\end{pmatrix} + \begin{pmatrix}-3\\-4\end{pmatrix} = \begin{pmatrix}8\\4\end{pmatrix}$
see diagram
c) $\begin{pmatrix}-1\\2\end{pmatrix} + \begin{pmatrix}8\\4\end{pmatrix} + \begin{pmatrix}-3\\-4\end{pmatrix} + \begin{pmatrix}-4\\-2\end{pmatrix} = \begin{pmatrix}0\\0\end{pmatrix}$

Q4 **a)** to **e)** — see diagram.

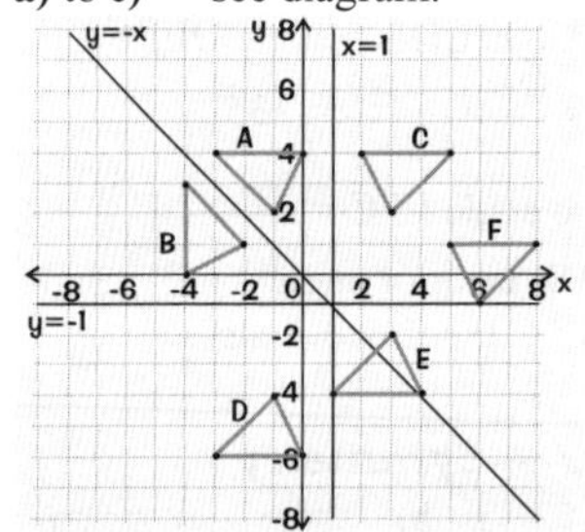

f) Rotation of +180° (or –180), centre (3, 0)

Q5 **a), b)** — see diagram.

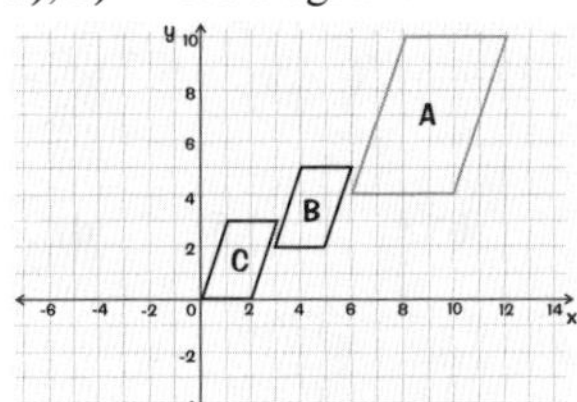

c) Ratio of areas C:A = 1:4

Pages 83-84 — Congruence, Similarity and Enlargement

Q1 **a)** Angle A shared. Parallel lines make corresponding angles equal so the triangles are similar.
b) Ratio of lengths given by $\frac{AB}{AD} = \frac{12}{20} = \frac{3}{5}$
So $x = 25 \times \frac{3}{5} = 15$ cm
Also $\frac{y+10}{y} = \frac{5}{3}$
$\Rightarrow 2y = 30, y = 15$ cm

Q2

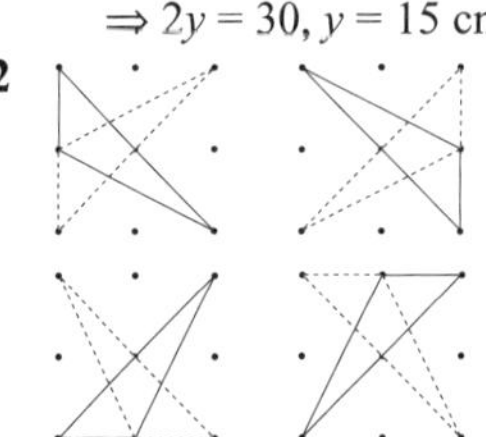

Hence 7 ways to draw another.

Q3 **a)** Triangles APQ and STC (both isosceles and share either angle A or C)
b) Ratio AC:AQ = 24:7.5 = 3.2:1 so
$AP = 15 \times \frac{1}{3.2} = 4.6875$ cm
PT = 24 – 2 (4.6875) = 14.625 cm
c) Using $\frac{1}{2}$(base)(height)
$= \frac{1}{2}(24)(9) = 108 \text{ cm}^2$
d) Scale factor = $\frac{1}{3.2}$
Area scale factor = $\frac{1}{10.24}$
Area of triangle APQ
$= 108 \times \frac{1}{10.24} = 10.5 \text{ cm}^2$
e) $108 - 2(10.5) = 87 \text{ cm}^2$

Q4 **a) & b)**

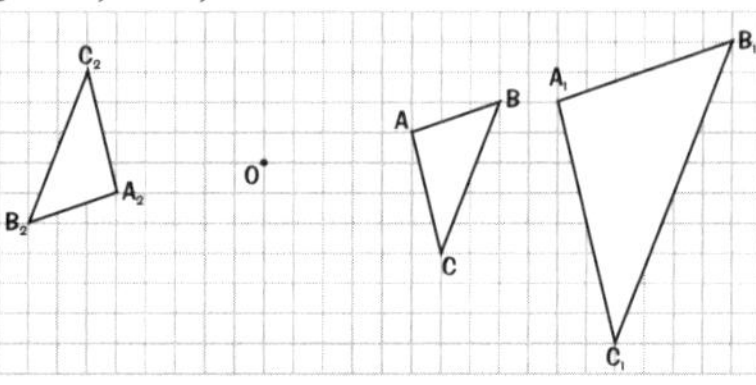

c) triangle $A_2B_2C_2$

Q5 Widths in ratio 2:3, so volumes in ratio 8:27.
Volume = $30 \times \frac{27}{8} = 101$ litres

Q6 **a)** All lengths must be enlarged in the same ratio for them to be similar.
b) 4 litres

Q7 **a)** 2 end faces 2 × (2 × 3) = 12 cm²
2 side faces 2 × (5 × 3) = 30 cm²
Top & bottom 2 × (5 × 2) = 20 cm²
Total = 62 cm²
b) SF for length = 1:4
SF for area = 1:16
new area = 62 × 16 = 992 cm²

Q8 **a)** volume = $\frac{1}{3}(\pi \times 100^2)(100)$
$= 1047198 \text{ cm}^3 = 1.05 \text{ m}^3$
b) 50 cm
c) ratio = $1:2^3 = 1:8$
d) Volume of small cone = $1.05 \times \frac{1}{8} = 0.131 \text{ m}^3$
e) volume of portion left = 1.05 – 0.131 = 0.919
so ratio = 0.919:0.131 = $\frac{0.919}{0.131}$:1
= 7:1

Pages 85-87 — Perimeter and Area

Q1 Area 24 cm², perimeter 20 cm
Q2 Area 25 cm², perimeter 20 cm
Q3 **a)** Area = $(4 \times 4) - (1 \times 2 + \frac{1}{2} \times \pi \times 1^2) + \frac{1}{2} \times \pi \times 2^2$
= 16 – 3.5708 + 6.2832
= 18.7 m² (1 d.p.)
b) Three 1 litre tins of paint are needed for two coats.
c) Perimeter = $1 + 1 + (\frac{1}{2} \times \pi \times 2) + 1 + 1 + 4 + (\frac{1}{2} \times \pi \times 4) + 4$
$= 12 + 3\pi = 21.4$ m (1 d.p.)
Q4 **a)** l = 24, w = 12, area = 288 m²

Answers: P85 — P91

b) 1 Carpet tile = 0.50×0.50 $= 0.25$ m^2
So 288 m^2 ÷ 0.25 = 1152 tiles are required.
c) £4.99 per m^2 => £4.99 for 4 tiles
Total cost = (1152 ÷ 4) × 4.99 = £1437.12

Q5 Area = 120 cm^2

Q6 Each square = 0.6 m × 0.6 m = 0.36 m^2.
Total area of material = 6 × 0.36 = 2.16 m^2

Q7 Perimeter = $4 \times \sqrt{9000}$ = 379.47 m (2 d.p.)
Natasha ran: 11 × 379.47 = 4200 m (to nearest 100 m)

Q8 48 ÷ 5 = 9.6 m length. Area of 1 roll = 11 m × 0.5 m = 5.5 m^2.
48 m^2 ÷ 5.5 m^2 = $8\frac{8}{11}$ rolls of turf required. Of course 9 should be ordered.

Q9 Base length = 4773 ÷ 43 = 111 mm.

Q10 Area of metal blade = ½ × 35 × (70 + 155) = 3937.5 mm^2

Q11 Area of larger triangle = ½ × 14.4 × 10 = 72 cm^2.
Area of inner triangle = ½ × 5.76 × 4 = 11.52 cm^2.
Area of metal used for a bracket = 72 – 11.52 = 60.48 cm^2 so NO, bracket is too heavy for the fixing.

Q12 T_1: ½ × 8 × 16 = 64 m^2
Tr_1: ½ × 8 × (8 + 16) = 96 m^2
Tr_2: ½ × 4 × (8 + 12) = 40 m^2
T_2: ½ × 8 × 12 = 48 m^2
Total area of glass sculpture = 248 m^2

Q13 Area = ½ × 8.2 × 4.1 = 16.81 m^2
Perimeter = 10.8 + 4.5 + 8.2 = 23.5 m.

Q14 **a)** Area of each isosceles triangle = ½ × 2.3 × 3.2 = 3.68 m^2
b) Area of each side = $(\sqrt{3.2^2 + 1.15^2}) \times 4 = 13.6$ m^2
Groundsheet = 2.3 × 4 = 9.2 m^2
c) Total material = 2 × 3.68 + 9.2 + 2 × 13.6 = 43.8 m^2

Q15

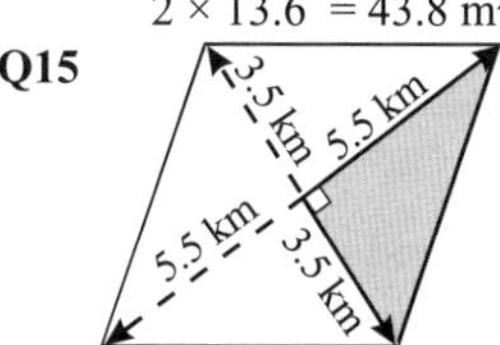

Area = ½ × product of diagonals = ½ × 7 × 11 = 38.5 km^2.

Q16 B = major sector
C = chord
D = tangent

Q17 **a)** 117.607 m^2 to 3 d.p.
b) 45.216 = 45 m to 2 s.f.
c) 46.5 m to 1 d.p.
d) 14.152 cm^2 to 3 d.p.
e) 12.0 cm^2 to 3 s.f.
f) 25.98 cm^2 to 2 d.p.

Q18 **a)** Area = area of a full circle radius 10 cm. A = πr^2 = 3.14 × 10^2 = 314 cm^2.
Circumference = π × D = 3.14 × 20 = 62.8 cm.
Perimeter = 62.8 + 20 = 82.8 cm
b) Area = (area of a full circle radius 15 cm) + (area of a rectangle 15 × 30 cm) = (π × 15^2) + (15 × 30) = 1156.5 cm^2.
Perimeter = (Circumference of a full circle radius 15 cm) + 15 +15 (two shorter sides of rectangle) = (π × 30) + 30 = 124.2 cm.
c) Area = Outer semi circle – Inner semi circle = 510.25 m^2.
Perimeter = ½ Circumference of larger + ½ Circumference of inner + 5 + 5 = ½ × π × 70 + ½ × π × 60 + 10 = 214.1 m.

Q19 **a)** ABDC = $\frac{60}{360} \times \pi(30)^2 - \frac{60}{360} \times \pi(20)^2$ = 261.8 mm^2
b) 2(½π5^2) = 78.5 mm^2.
Hence 261.8 + 78.5 = 340.3 mm^2.

Q20 **a)** 80/360 × π5^2 = 17.45 cm^2
b) Area of triangle AOB = $\frac{1}{2} \times 5 \times 5 \times \sin 80°$ = 12.31 cm^2
Shaded Area = 17.45 – 12.31 = 5.14 cm^2

Pages 88-89 — Surface Area

Q1 **a) - c)**

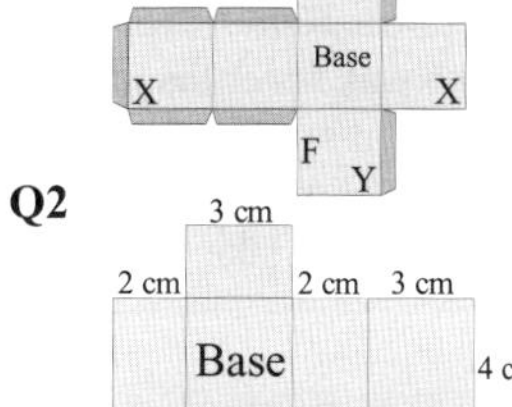

Q2

3 cm
2 cm | 2 cm | 3 cm
Base | 4 cm

Other arrangements are possible.

Q3 **a)** H, F and D
b) Line symmetry through lines AF, DH, BG and CE. Rotational symmetry of order 4.
c) 5 faces and vertices, 8 edges.

Q4 **a)** I
b) 64 cm^2
c) 64 × 6 = 384 cm^2
d)

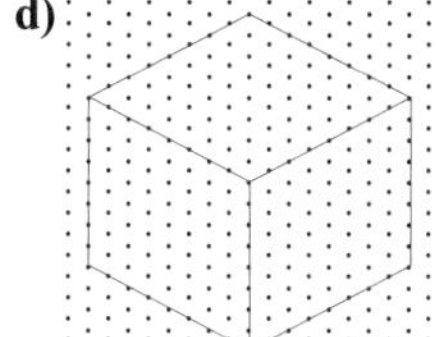

Q5 Net B

Q6 No, Hannah would need more than 603 cm^2.

Q7 Surface area = 4 × π × 3^2 = 113.10 cm^2 (to 2 d.p)

Q8 Surface area of cone = $\pi rl + \pi r^2$
= (π × 1.5 × 8) + (π × 1.5^2)
= 44.77 cm^2 (to 2 d.p)
Height of triangular prism = $\sqrt{3^2 - 1.5^2}$ = $\sqrt{6.75}$ = 2.598... cm
Surface area of triangular prism = $2(\frac{1}{2} \times 3 \times 2.598...) + 3(3 \times 8)$ = 79.79 cm^2 (to 2 d.p.)
Therefore the triangular prism has the largest surface area.

Q9 Surface area of hemisphere = $\pi r^2 + \frac{1}{2}(4\pi r^2)$
$75\pi = 3\pi r^2$
$r^2 = 25$, radius = 5 cm

Q10 AB^2 = 2^2 + 1.5^2 AB = 2.5 m
1 panel on roof = ½AB × $\frac{5}{2}$ = 1.25 × 2.5 = 3.125 m^2
Front of greenhouse = (2.5 × 4) + (½ × 4 × 1.5) = 13 m^2
Total = 3.125 + 13 = 16.125 m^2

Pages 90-92 — Volume

Q1 **a)** $\frac{1}{2}\pi(0.35)^2 = 0.192$ m^2
b) 0.1924 × 3 = 0.577 m^3

Q2 **a)** π(2.5^2 – 2^2) = 7.07 m^2
£16 × 7.07 = £113.12 = £110 to nearest £10.
b) Volume = π(2)^2 × 0.50 = 6.28 m^3 so use 6.28 × 15 = 94 ml treatment to the nearest ml.

Q3 **a)** Volume Cube = Volume Cylinder
$10^3 = \pi r^2 \times 10$ so $r^2 = \frac{10^2}{\pi}$, r = 5.64 cm
b) S.A. of cylinder = $2\pi rh + 2\pi r^2$ = 2π × 5.64... × 10 + 2π × (5.64...)^2 = 554.49 cm^2

Q4 **a)** π(5)^2(16) = 1257 cm^3
b) $\pi(5)^2h = 600$
$h = \frac{600}{25\pi}$ = 7.64 cm

Q5 (3)(3)(0.5) – π(0.7)^2(0.5) = 3.73 cm^3

Q6 Volume = $\frac{1}{3} \times (230 \times 230) \times 139$ = 2 451 033 m^3

Q7 (π × (2)^2 × 110) + (½(14 + 20) × 6 × 20) = 3422.30 cm^3
2 × 3422.30 = 6844.60 cm^3 = 6.84 l

Q8 **a)** (60)(30) + (30)(120) = 5400 cm^2
b) 5400 × 100 = 540000 cm^3 = 0.54 m^3

Q9 Volume = $\frac{4}{3}\pi r^3 = \frac{4}{3} \times \pi \times 15^3$ = 14137 cm^3

Q10 $\frac{\text{volume of cylinder}}{\text{volume of hemisphere}} = \frac{\pi r^2 h}{\frac{1}{2} \times \frac{4}{3}\pi r^3}$
$= \frac{6\pi r^2 h}{4\pi r^3} = \frac{3h}{2r}$
$\frac{3h}{2r} = 3 \Rightarrow h = 2r$

Answers: P92 — P98

Q11 a) $\frac{1}{2}(\frac{4}{3}\pi(1.3)^3) + \pi(1.3)^2 \times 1.8 + \frac{1}{3}\pi(1.3)^2 \times 1.2 = 16.28 \text{ cm}^3$

b) Volume of sand in hemisphere and cone parts remain the same so change is in cylindrical part. Therefore $h + 0.3 = 1.8$, $h = 1.5$ cm.

c) Volume of sand transferred = $\frac{1}{2}(\frac{4}{3}\pi(1.3)^3) + \pi(1.3)^2 \times 1.5 = 12.57 \text{ cm}^3$

Time Taken = $\frac{12.57}{0.05} \approx 251$ secs. = 4 minutes 11 secs

Q12 a) Volume of ice cream

$= \frac{1}{3}\pi(R^2H - r^2h) + \frac{1}{2}(\frac{4}{3}\pi R^3)$

$= \frac{1}{3}\pi(2.5^2 \times 10 - 1^2 \times 4) + \frac{1}{2}(\frac{4}{3}\pi \times 2.5^3)$

$= 93.99 \text{ cm}^3$ of ice cream.

b) Outer surface area of cone $= \pi Rl$

Using Pythagoras, $l^2 = 10^2 + 2.5^2 = 106.25$, $l = 10.3$ cm. So S.A. = $\pi \times 2.5 \times 10.3 = 81.0 \text{ cm}^2$

Q13 Vol. increase is a cylinder of height 4.5 cm. So vol. increase = $\pi(5)^2 \times 4.5 = 353.4 \text{ cm}^3$.

Volume of each marble = $\frac{353.4}{200} = 1.767 \text{ cm}^3$

$\frac{4}{3}\pi r^3 = 1.767 \Rightarrow r = 0.75$ cm

Q14 a) $x(3 - x)(5 - x) \text{ m}^3$ or $x^3 - 8x^2 + 15x$

b)

X	0	1	2	3
V	0	8	6	0

c)

d) about 8.2 m^3

e)

ends	2(1.2)(1.8) =	4.32 +
side faces	2(1.2)(3.8) =	9.12 +
tops	2(3.8)(1.8) =	13.68
So area is about		27.12 m^2

f) $x = 2$ or $x = 0.6$

If $x = 0.6$:

ends	2(0.6)(2.4) =	2.88 +
side faces	2(0.6)(4.4) =	5.28 +
tops	2(2.4)(4.4) =	21.12
		29.28 m^2

If $x = 2$:

ends	2(2)(1) =	4 +
side faces	2(2)(3) =	12 +
tops	2(1)(3) =	6
		22 m^2

Maximum Total S.A. $\approx 29.28 \text{ m}^2$

Page 93 — Time

Q1 **a)** 5 am **b)** 2.48 pm **c)** 3.16 am **d)** 3.58 pm **e)** 10.30 pm **f)** 12.01 am

Q2 **a)** 2330 **b)** 1022 **c)** 0015 **d)** 1215 **e)** 0830 **f)** 1645

Q3 145 mins

Q4 **a)** 8 hours **b)** 10 hours **c)** 11 hrs 56 mins **d)** 47 hrs 48 mins

Q5 **a)** 3 hrs 15 mins **b)** 24 mins **c)** 7 hrs 18 mins **d)** 1 hr 12 mins

Q6 **a)** 2.33 hrs **b)** 3.1 hrs **c)** 0.33 hrs

Q7 **a)** Train 3 **b)** Train 1 **c)** 1208

Pages 94-96 — Speed, Density and Pressure

Q1 **a)** 100/11= 9.09 m/s (to 2 d.p) **b)** 32.73 km/h

Q2 540 km/h

Q3 Journey takes 3 hrs 39 mins. 07.05 to 10.30 is 3 hrs 25 mins. So Pete will not be in London on time.

Q4 **a)** 98.9 km/h **b)** 72.56 s **c)** 99.2 km/h

Q5 **a)** 5 hrs 31 mins 30 s **b)** 405 km **c)** 73.3 km/h

Q6 2.15pm

Q7 **a)** 2.23 hrs (2 hrs 14 mins) **b)** 1 hr 49 mins + 10 mins = 1 hr 59 mins **c)** 1346 and 1401

Q8 The first athlete ran at 16000 ÷ (60 × 60) = 4.44 m/s, so was faster than the second athlete (at 4 m/s). The first athlete would take 37.5 mins to run 10 km; the second would take 41.7 mins.

Q9 **a)** 487.5 km **b)** 920.8 km **c)** 497.1 km/h

Q10 **a)** 8.13 m/s **b)** 7.30 m/s

Q11 **a)** 220 km **b)** 5 mins

Q12 1 hr 27 mins.

Q13 **a)** 4.9 m/s **b)** 24.5 m/s **c)** 14.7 m/s **d)** 17.64 km/h, 88.2 km/h, 52.92 km/h.

Q14 **a)** 0.75 g/cm^3 **b)** 0.6 g/cm^3 **c)** 0.8 g/cm^3 **d)** $700 \text{ kg/m}^3 = 0.7 \text{ g/cm}^3$

Q15 **a)** 62.4 g **b)** 96 g **c)** 3744 g (3.744 kg) **d)** 75 g

Q16 **a)** 1176 cm^3 **b)** 278 cm^3 (to 3 s.f.) **c)** 2500 cm^3 **d)** $45\,500 \text{ cm}^3$ (to 3 s.f.)

Q17 34.71 g

Q18 20968 cm^3

Q19 Vol. = 5000 cm^3 = 5 litres

Q20 1.05 g/cm^3

Q21 **a)** SR flour 1.16 g/cm^3; granary flour 1.19 g/cm^3 **b)** 378 ml

Q22 165.23 g

Q23 150 N/m^2

Q24 0.8 m^2

Q25 448 N

Q26 30.59 cm

Pages 97-98 — D/T and S/T Graphs

Q1 **a)** 4 km **b)** 15 mins and 45 mins **c)** 2.4 km/h **d)** 1100 **e)** 10 km/h **f)** 1030

Q2 **a)** 1 hr 25 mins **b)** 1 hr 15 mins **c)** 25.4 km/h **d)** 86.4 km/h **e)** No. Can't get to Ingleton and back.

Q3 **a)** A 80.0 km/h, fastest.
B 57.1 km/h
C 66.7 km/h
D 44.4 km/h
E 50.0 km/h

b) steepest slope was fastest, least steep slope was slowest.

Q4

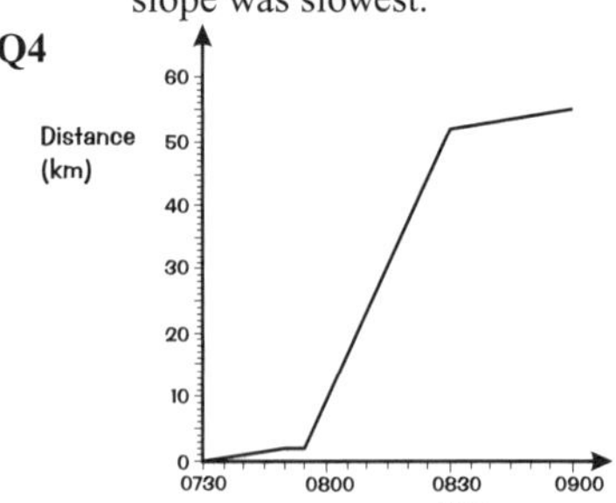

He waited for 5 mins.

Q5 **a)** 3 hours **b)** 4 to 6 hours into the journey **c)** Travelling at a constant speed of 15 km/h

Q6 **a)** acceleration = change in speed ÷ time = $(100 - 60)/1 = 40 \text{ km/h}^2$ **b)** The first hour.

Q7 **a)**

b) accept 1243-1245

c) accept 35-36 km

Answers: P98 — P105

Q8 a)

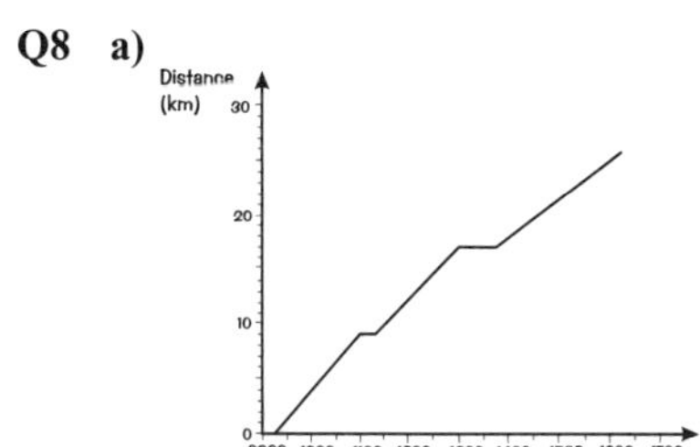

b) 25.75 km **c)** 3.68 km/h

d) Her fastest speed was in the first section (steepest graph) — her speed was 5.14 km/h.

Page 99 — Unit Conversions

Q1 **a)** 200 cm **i)** 6000 mm
b) 33 mm **j)** 2000 kg
c) 4000 g **k)** 3 kg
d) 0.6 kg **l)** 86 mm
e) 0.65 km **m)** 0.55 tonnes
f) 9000 g **n)** 354 cm
g) 0.007 kg **o)** 7 mm
h) 0.95 kg **p)** 4.2 l

Q2 **a)** 0.47 m **b)** 470 mm

Q3 **a)** 300 cm **c)** 0.003 km
b) 3000 mm

Q4 **a)** 0.2 km **c)** 7 km
b) 2 km **d)** 0.02 km^2

Q5 **a)** 167 cm **c)** 0.11 cm^2
b) 33.3 cm **d)** 0.056 cm^2

Q6 **a)** £4.69 **b)** £51.07

Page 100 — Conversion Graphs

Q1 **a) i)** £5 **ii)** £9.50 **iii)** £17
b) No (each 4.5 km journey costs more than £8)

Q2 **a)** \$4.50 **c)** £2
b) \$2.25 **d)** £3.65 (+/– £0.05)

Q3 **a) i)** 12-13 miles
ii) 43-44 miles
iii) 56-57 miles
b) i) 63-65 km
ii) 15-17 km
iii) 47-49 km

Page 101 — Constructions

Q1

Not to scale

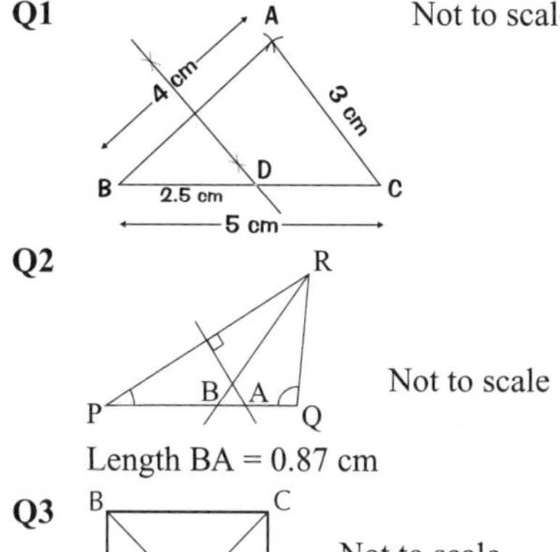

Q2

Not to scale

Length BA = 0.87 cm

Q3

Not to scale

Q4

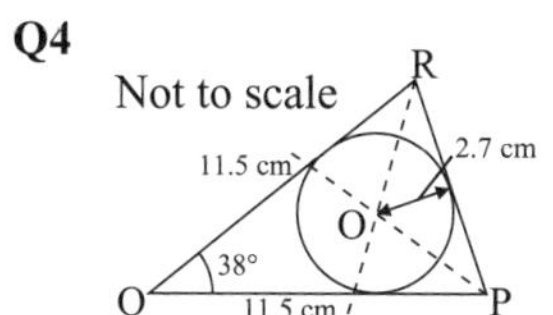

Radius of the circle = 2.7 cm

Page 102 — Bearings

Q1 **a)** 245° **b)** 310°
c) 035° **d)** 131°
e) 297°, 028°, 208°

Q2 **a)**

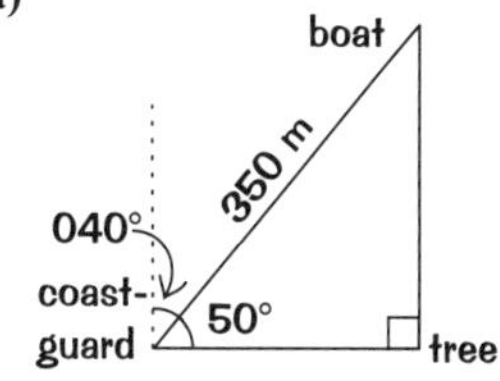

i) 268 m
ii) 225 m

b) $350^2 = 122\ 500$.
$225^2 + 268^2 = 122\ 449$

Q3

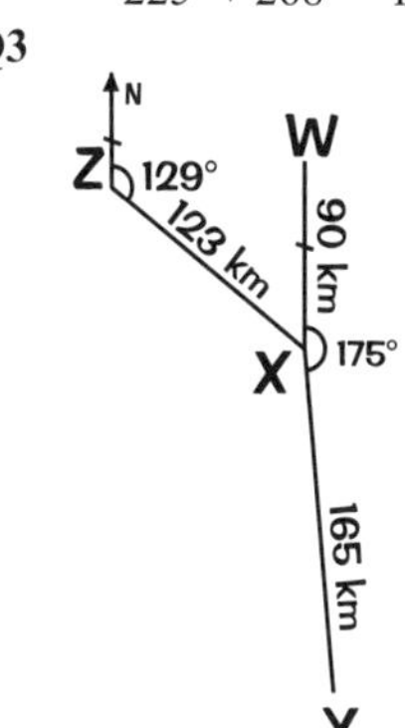

a) 96 km
b) 255 km
c) 266 km
d) 156°
e) 082°
f) 177°

Q4

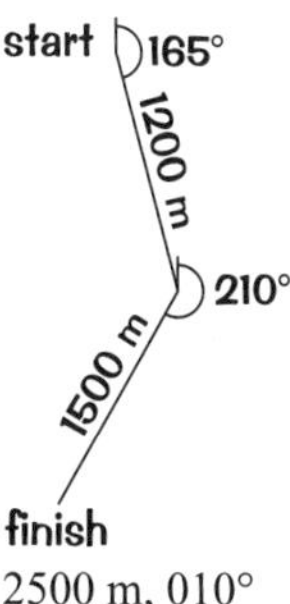

2500 m, 010°

Section Five — Pythagoras and Trigonometry

Pages 103-105 — Pythagoras' Theorem

Q1 **a)** 10.8 cm **f)** 7.89 m
b) 6.10 m **g)** 9.60 cm
c) 5 cm **h)** 4.97 cm
d) 27.0 mm **i)** 6.80 cm
e) 8.49 m **j)** 8.5 cm

Q2 a = 3.32 cm f = 8.62 m
b = 6 cm g = 6.42 m
c = 6.26 m h = 19.2 mm
d = 5.6 mm i = 9.65 m
e = 7.08 mm j = 48.7 mm

Q3 k = 6.55 cm q = 7.07 cm
l = 4.87 m r = 7.50 m
m = 6.01 m s = 9.45 mm
n = 12.4 cm t = 4.33 cm
p = 5.22 cm u = 7.14 m

Q4 9.7 m

Q5 **a)** 12 cm, 7.94 cm
b) 40.9 cm
c) 89.7 cm^2

Q6 314 m

Q7 91.9 cm

Q8 5.0 m

Q9 4.58 m

Q10 AB: 5 (don't need Pythagoras)
CD: $\sqrt{10} = 3.16$
EF: $\sqrt{13} = 3.61$
GH: $\sqrt{8} = 2.83$
JK: $\sqrt{5} = 2.24$
LM: $\sqrt{26} = 5.10$
PQ: $\sqrt{20} = 4.47$
RS: $\sqrt{45} = 6.71$
TU: $\sqrt{13} = 3.61$

Q11 **a) i)** 5
ii) $\sqrt{17} = 4.12$
iii) 5
iv) $\sqrt{58} = 7.62$
v) $\sqrt{26} = 5.10$
b) parallelogram

Q12 **a)** $\sqrt{41} = 6.40$
b) $\sqrt{98} = 9.90$
c) $\sqrt{53} = 7.28$
d) $\sqrt{34} = 5.83$
e) 4 (don't need Pythagoras here)
f) $\sqrt{37} = 6.08$

Q13 **a)** $\sqrt{10} = 3.16$
b) $\sqrt{130} = 11.40$
c) $\sqrt{8} = 2.83$
d) $\sqrt{233} = 15.26$
e) $\sqrt{353} = 18.79$
f) $\sqrt{100} = 10$

Q14 192 km

Answers: P105 — P110

Q15

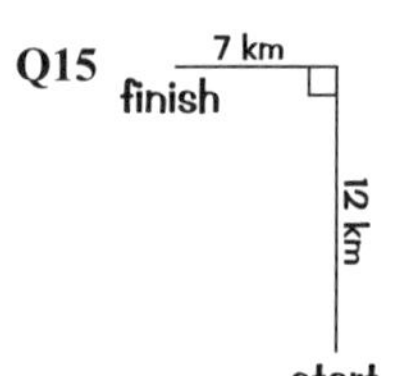

13.9 km from the starting point.
150° to return to base.

Pages 106-108 — Trigonometry — Sin, Cos, Tan

		(tan)	(sin)	(cos)
Q1	**a)**	0.306	0.292	0.956
	b)	8.14	0.993	0.122
	c)	0.0875	0.0872	0.996
	d)	0.532	0.469	0.883
	e)	1	0.707	0.707

Q2 a = 1.40 cm c = 5.31 cm
b = 6 cm d = 10.8 cm
θ = 28.1°

Q3 e = 12.6 cm g = 6.71 m
f = 11.3 cm h = 30.1 cm
θ = 49.5°

Q4 i = 4.89 cm k = 5.32 cm
j = 3.79 cm l = 41.6 cm
θ = 52.4°

Q5 m = 11.3 cm t = 59.8 cm
n = 18.8 cm u = 14.5 cm
p = 8.62 cm v = 11.7 cm
q = 21.3 cm w = 11.7 cm
r = 54.6°

Q6 a)

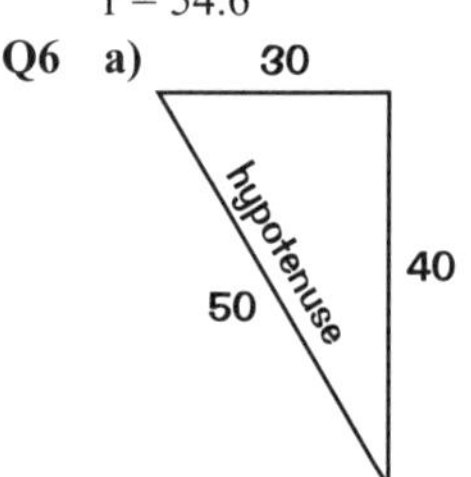

b) 36.9°

Q7 a)

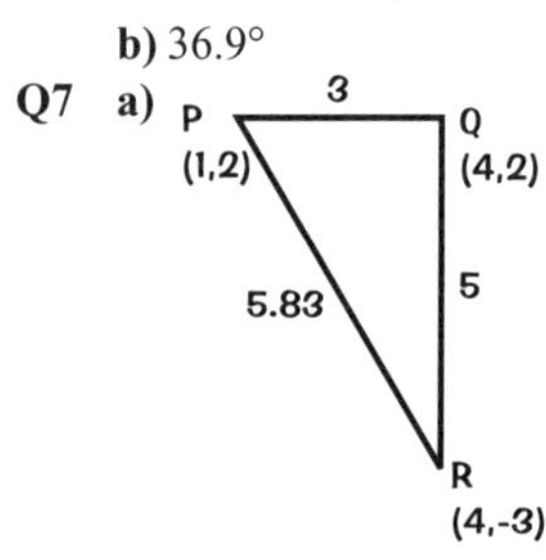

b) 59.0°
c) 31.0°

Q8 a)

b) 71.6°
c) 36.9°
d) 71.5°

Q9 2.1 m
Q10 62°
Q11 20.5°
Q12

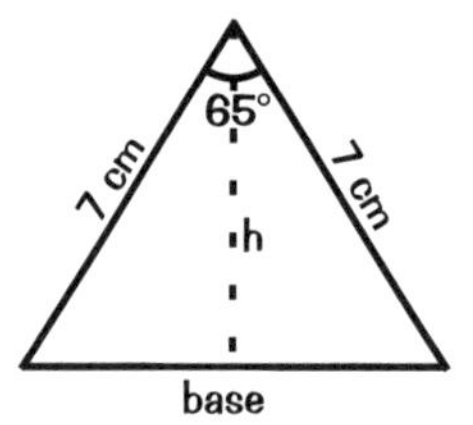

θ = 52.1°, bearing = 322°

Q13 a) both 30.8 cm
b) 27.5 cm **c)** 385 cm²

Q14

height = 5.90, base = 7.52,
so area = 22.2 cm².

Q15 a) 8.23 cm
b) 4.75 cm **c)** 39.1 cm²

Q16 a) 10.8 cm
b) 150.8 cm² **c)** 21.0°

Q17

750 m

Q18

25.8 m

Q19

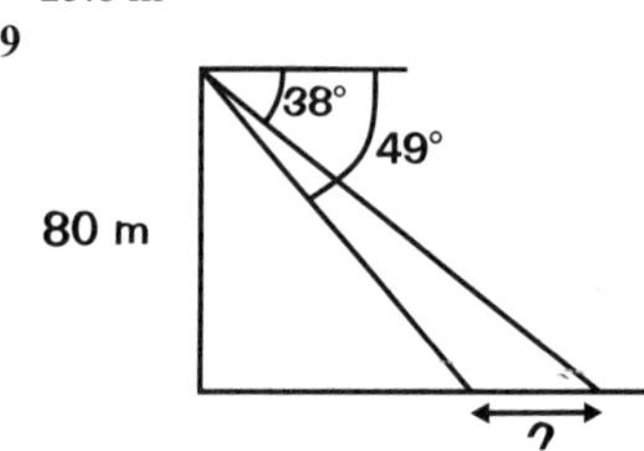

a) 102.4 m, 69.5 m
b) 32.9 m

Q20

86.6 km

Pages 109-110 — The Sine and Cosine Rules

Q1 a = 4.80 cm f = 5.26 cm
b = 25.8 mm g = 9.96 cm
c = 13.0 cm h = 20.2 mm
d = 8.89 m i = 3.72 m
e = 18.4 cm j = 8.29 cm

Q2 k = 51° r = 64°
l = 46° s = 18°
m = 43° t = 49°
p = 45° u = 88°
q = 36°

Q3 a) 46°
b) 52° **c)** 82°

Q4 a) 18.1 cm² **d)** 29.5 m²
b) 8.5 m² **e)** 25.5 cm²
c) 198.6 cm² **f)** 17.4 mm²

Q5 a) 28.8 km **b)** 295.5°

Q6

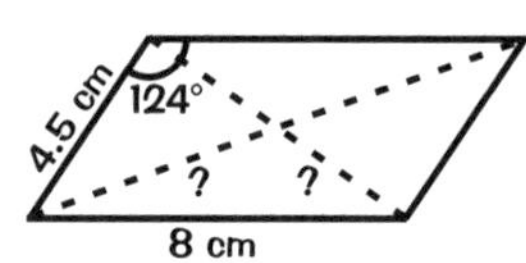

Diagonals 11.2 cm and 6.6 cm.

Q7

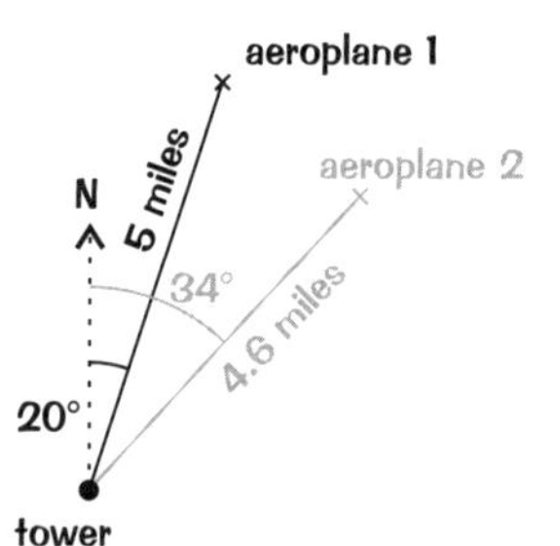

Distance = 1.2 miles.
The alarm should be ringing because the planes are less than 3 miles apart, so the software seems reliable.

Q8 a) 16.9 m **b)** 12.4 m
c) 25.8 m **d)** 19.5 m

Q9

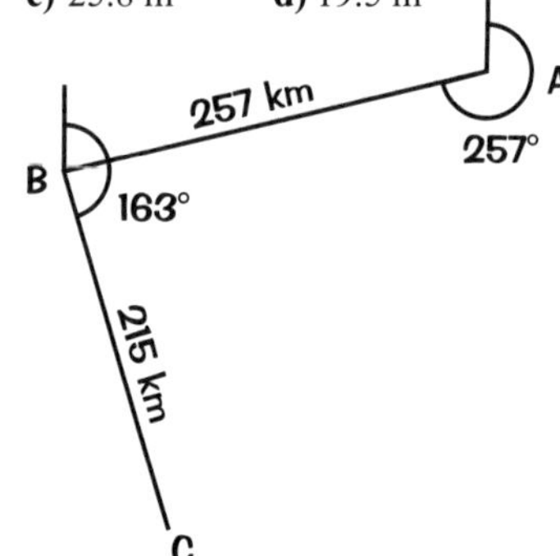

Answers: P110 — P116

a) 86°
b) 323 km
c) 215°

Q10 a)

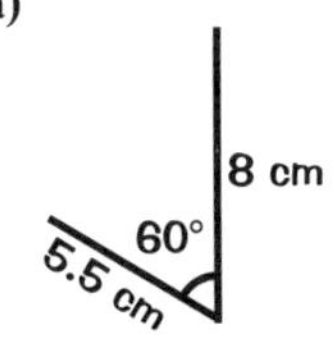

7.1 cm

b)

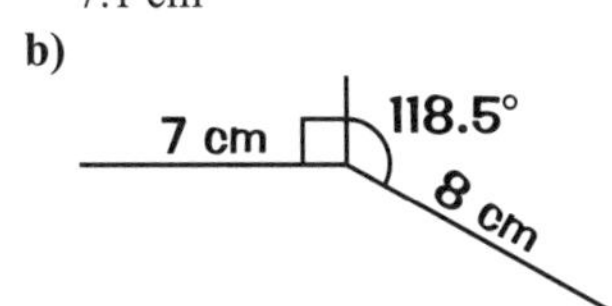

14.5 cm
(118.5° comes from the fact that the minute hand is at 19.75 mins. 19.75 ÷ 60 × 360 = 118.5.)

c)

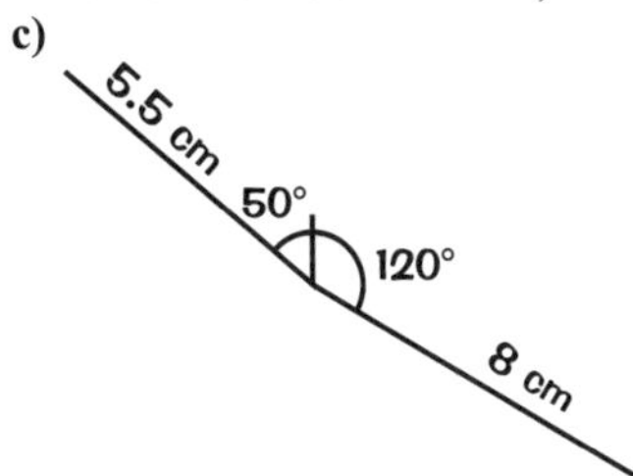

13.5 cm

Q11 Height of building = 35 m

Q12

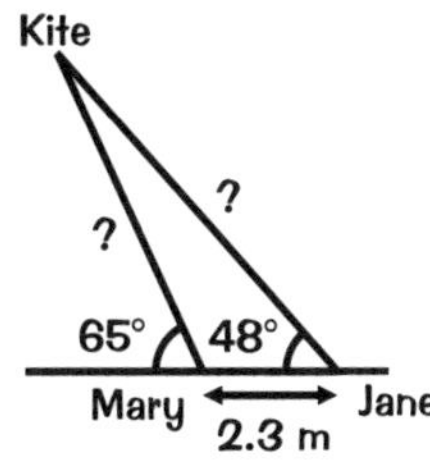

Mary's string = 5.85 m
Jane's string = 7.13 m

Page 111 — 3D Pythagoras and Trigonometry

Q1 **a)** 59.0° **c)** 25 cm
b) 23.3 cm **d)** 21.1°
Q2 **a)** 42.5 cm **b)** 50.9 cm
Q3 **a)** 36.1 cm, 21.5 cm, 31.0 cm
b) 36.9 cm
Q4 **a)** 15.4 cm **b)** 20.4 cm
Q5 The 85p box
Q6 **a)** 3.82 cm
b) 45.8 cm²
c) 137.5 cm³

Page 112 — Sin, Cos and Tan for Larger Angles

Q1 a = 5.7 cm e = 13.0 cm
B = 38.9° F = 62.6°
c = 8.2 cm G = 115.4°
D = 140°
Q2 **a)** 122.9° **c)** 135°
b) 170.0° **d)** 94.0°

Q3 32.1 m
Q4 **a)** 109°
b) Front = 28.5 m, roof = 107.6 m
c) 24.2 m
Q5 24.6 km
Q6 42.5° and 137.5°
Q7 153.5°

Pages 113-114 — Vectors

Q1 **a)**

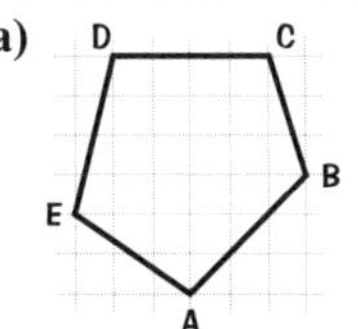

b) i) $\begin{pmatrix}-1\\-4\end{pmatrix}$ **ii)** $\begin{pmatrix}4\\0\end{pmatrix}$ **iii)** $\begin{pmatrix}5\\4\end{pmatrix}$
c) Isosceles

Q2 **a)**

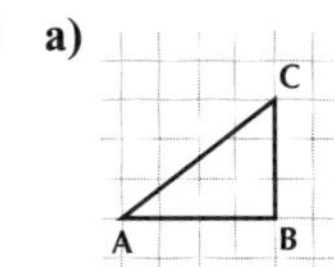

b) Using Pythagoras,
$|\overrightarrow{\mathbf{AC}}| = \sqrt{4^2 + 3^2} = 5$

Q3 **a)** $\begin{pmatrix}2\\1\end{pmatrix}$ p+q

b) $\begin{pmatrix}2\\5\end{pmatrix}$

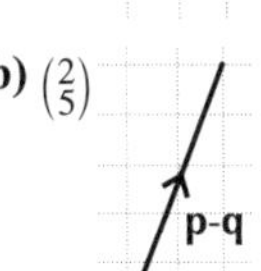

c) $\begin{pmatrix}6\\-2\end{pmatrix}$ 2r

d) $\begin{pmatrix}1\\1\end{pmatrix}$ s+p

e) $\begin{pmatrix}6\\10\end{pmatrix}$

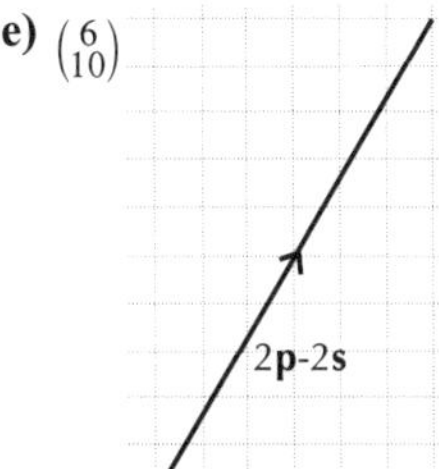

f) $\begin{pmatrix}-1\\-8\end{pmatrix}$

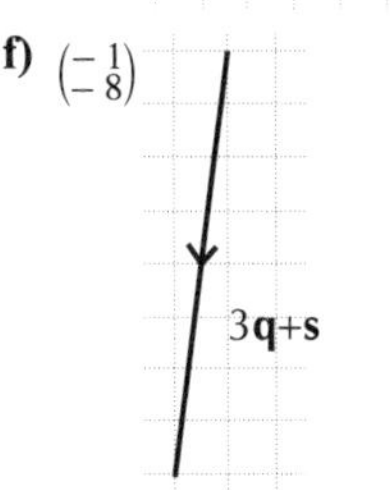

g) $\begin{pmatrix}6\\0\end{pmatrix}$ 2r-q

h) $\begin{pmatrix}6\\-3\end{pmatrix}$ ½q+2r

i) $\begin{pmatrix}0\\-1\end{pmatrix}$ p+2s

j) $\begin{pmatrix}-6\\0\end{pmatrix}$

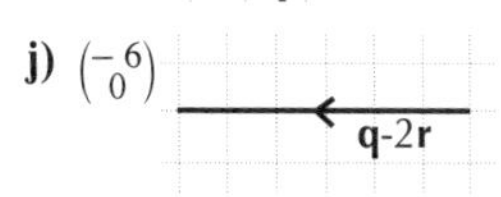

Q4 **a)** 1 **f)** 5
b) 3.61 **g)** 8.60
c) 1 **h)** 8.49
d) 3.61 **i)** 9.43
e) 6.08 **j)** 11.18
Q5 **a)** $\begin{pmatrix}3\\3\end{pmatrix}$ **d)** 5.39
b) 4.24 **e)** $\begin{pmatrix}2\\-2\end{pmatrix}$
c) $\begin{pmatrix}5\\-2\end{pmatrix}$ **f)** 2.83
Q6 **a)** $2y$ **d)** $2y + 2x$
b) $y + x$ **e)** $4y + 2x$
c) $-y - x$ **f)** $2x$
Q7 **a) i)** $\overrightarrow{ED}$ or $\overrightarrow{AF}$ **v)** $\overrightarrow{BE}$
ii) $\overrightarrow{EF}$ or $\overrightarrow{DC}$ **vi)** $\overrightarrow{AC}$
iii) $\overrightarrow{AE}$ **vii)** $\overrightarrow{EC}$ or $\overrightarrow{AB}$
iv) $\overrightarrow{BA}$ **viii)** $\overrightarrow{EB}$
b) i) 48 cm² **ii)** 60 cm²
Q8 $\overrightarrow{EG} = -\frac{3}{5}\underset{\sim}{a} + \frac{6}{5}\underset{\sim}{b}$
Q9 **a) i)** 2**a** **ii)** **b** − 2**a** **iii)** **a** − **b**
b) $\overrightarrow{AC}$ = −2**b** + 2**a** = 2(**a** − **b**).
Since $\overrightarrow{AC}$ is a multiple of $\overrightarrow{PQ}$, they must both be in the same direction and therefore parallel.

Section Six — Statistics and Probability

Pages 115-116 — Mean, Median, Mode and Range

Q1 3 tries
Q2 mean = 1.333 (to 3 dp)
median = 1.5
mode = 2
range = 11
Q3 **a)** mean = £12,944, or £13,000 to the nearest £500
median = £12,000
mode = £7,500
b) mode
c) E.g. mean — they should use the highest value to attract people to the job.
Q4 **a)** 0 minutes **b)** 0 minutes
c) 0 minutes
d) No, according to the raw data.
Q5 73.5 kg
Q6 20 kg
Q7 97%
Q8 **a)** 22 **b)** 74
Q9 **a)** 3.5 **b)** 3.5 **c)** 5

Answers: P116 — P122

Q10 **a)** Both spend a mean of 2 hours.
b) The range for Jim is 3 hours and for Bob is 2 hours.
c) The amount of TV that Jim watches each night is more variable than the amount that Bob watches.

Q11 **a)** 1 day
b) 2 days
c) The statement is true according to the data.

Q12 **a)** mode
b) median **c)** mean

Page 117 — Quartiles and Comparing Distributions

Q1 **a)** 65 g **b)** The 2nd quartile (or Q_2)

Q2 **a)** 1020 – 80 = 940
b) 510 **c)** 700 **d)** 840

Q3 200

Q4 **a)** 325 **b)** 50

Q5 Mean (before)
= 3·61 fillings per child
Mean (after)
= 2·08 fillings per child
Mode (before)
= 4 fillings per child
Mode (after)
= 2 fillings per child
(all other things being equal, I'd say that the dental hygienist has decreased the number of fillings received by each child.)

Pages 118-119 — Frequency Tables — Finding Averages

Q1 **a)** 12 **b)** 12 **c)** 2

Q2 **a)**

Subject	M	E	F	A	S
Frequency	5	7	3	4	6

b) 36 French lessons **c)** English

Q3

Length (m)	4 and under	6	8	10	12	14 and over
Frequency	3	5	6	4	1	1

a) 8 m **b)** 8 m **c)** 14 m

Q4

Weight (kg)	Frequency	Weight × Frequency
51	40	2040
52	30	1560
53	45	2385
54	10	540
55	5	275

a) 52 kg **b)** 2 kg
c) 53 kg **d)** 52 kg (to nearest kg)

Q5 mean = 3.75
mode = 3
median = 4

Q6 **a)** 4 **b)** 3 **c)** 3.2 (to 1 dp)

Q7 **a)** **i)** False, mode is 8.
ii) False, they are equal.
iii) True
b) iv)

Page 120 — Grouped Frequency Tables

Q1 **a)**

Speed (km/h)	40≤s<45	45≤s<50	50≤s<55	55≤s<60	60≤s<65
Frequency	4	8	10	7	3
Mid-Interval	42.5	47.5	52.5	57.5	62.5
Frequency × Mid-Interval	170	380	525	402.5	187.5

Estimated mean = 52 km/h (to nearest km/h)
b) 22 skiers **c)** 20 skiers

Q2 **a)**

Weight (kg)	Tally	Frequency	Mid-Interval	Frequency × Mid-Interval
200≤w<250	IIII	4	225	900
250≤w<300	~~IIII~~	5	275	1375
300≤w<350	~~IIII~~ II	7	325	2275
350≤w<400	II	2	375	750

b) 294 kg (to nearest kg)
c) 300 ⩽ w < 350 kg

Q3 **a)**

Number	0≤n<0.2	0.2≤n<0.4	0.4≤n<0.6	0.6≤n<0.8	0.8≤n<1
Tally	~~IIII~~ ~~IIII~~ II	~~IIII~~ I	~~IIII~~ ~~IIII~~ II	~~IIII~~ ~~IIII~~	~~IIII~~ III
Frequency	12	6	12	10	8
Mid-Interval	0.1	0.3	0.5	0.7	0.9
Frequency × Mid-Interval	1.2	1.8	6	7	7.2

b) 0 ⩽ n < 0.2 and 0.4 ⩽ n < 0.6
c) 0.4 ⩽ n < 0.6
d) 0.483 (3 dp)

Pages 121-122 — Cumulative Frequency

Q1 accept:
a) 133-134 **c)** 136-137
b) 127-128 **d)** 8-10

Q2 **a)**

Number of passengers	0≤n<50	50≤n<100	100≤n<150	150≤n<200	200≤n<250	250≤n<300
Frequency	2	7	10	5	3	1
Cumulative Frequency	2	9	19	24	27	28
Mid-Interval	25	75	125	175	225	275
Frequency × Mid-Interval	50	525	1250	875	675	275

Estimated mean = 130 passengers (to nearest whole number)

b)

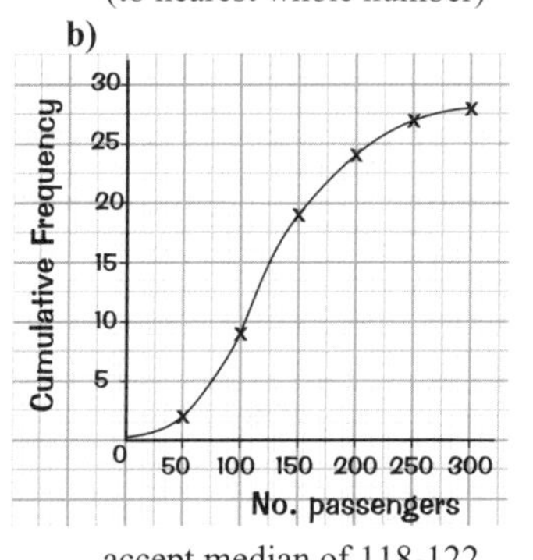

accept median of 118-122 passengers

c) 100 ⩽ n < 150

Q3 **a)**

Mark (%)	0≤m<20	20≤m<40	40≤m<60	60≤m<80	80≤m<100
Frequency	2	12	18	5	3
Cumulative Frequency	2	14	32	37	40

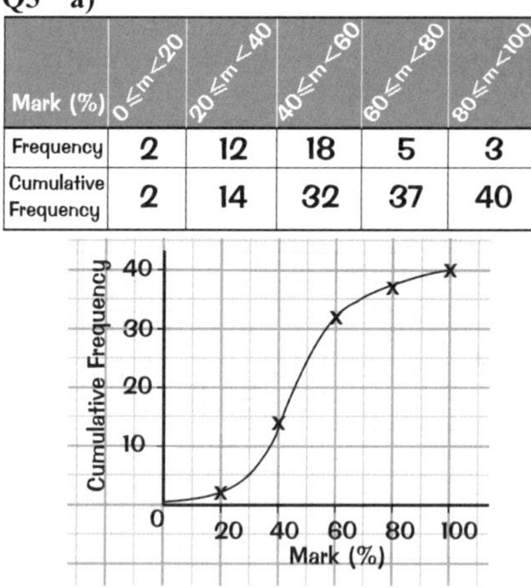

b) 36%-38%
c) 19%-21%
d) 45%-47%

Q4

Score	31≤s<41	41≤s<51	51≤s<61	61≤s<71	71≤s<81	81≤s<91	91≤s<101
Frequency	4	12	21	32	19	8	4
Cumulative frequency	4	16	37	69	88	96	100

a) 61 ⩽ s < 71
b) 61 ⩽ s < 71
c)

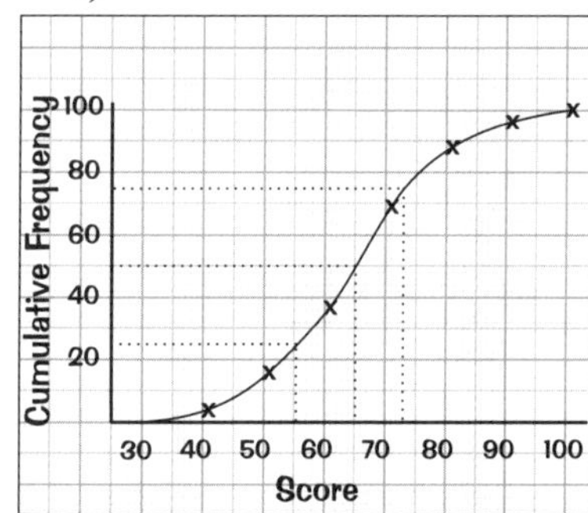

median = 65 (accept 64-66)
d) 73 – 55 = 18 (accept 17-19)

Q5 **a)**

Life (hours)	Frequency	Cumulative Frequency
900 ≤ L < 1000	10	10
1000 ≤ L < 1100	12	22
1100 ≤ L < 1200	15	37
1200 ≤ L < 1300	18	55
1300 ≤ L < 1400	22	77
1400 ≤ L < 1500	17	94
1500 ≤ L < 1600	14	108
1600 ≤ L < 1700	9	117

b) 1300 ⩽ L < 1400

Answers: P122 — P127

c)

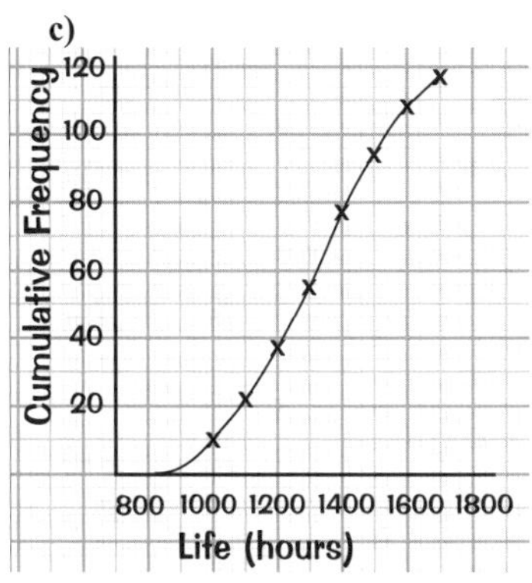

median = 1320 hours (±20)

d) lower quartile = 1150 (±20)
upper quartile = 1460 (±20)

Q6 a)

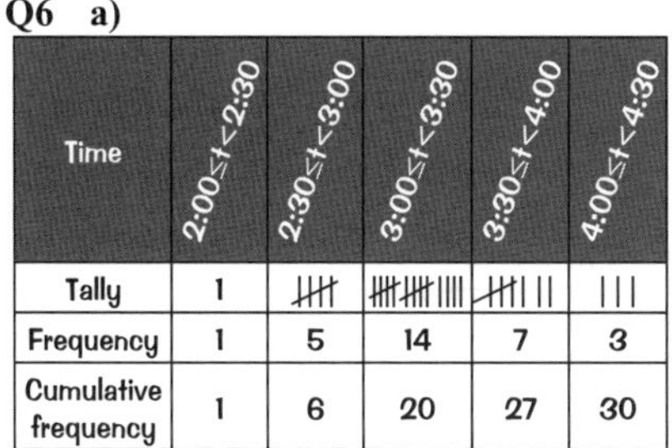

Time	2:00≤t<2:30	2:30≤t<3:00	3:00≤t<3:30	3:30≤t<4:00	4:00≤t<4:30
Tally	|	卌	卌 卌 ||||	卌 ||	|||
Frequency	1	5	14	7	3
Cumulative frequency	1	6	20	27	30

b)

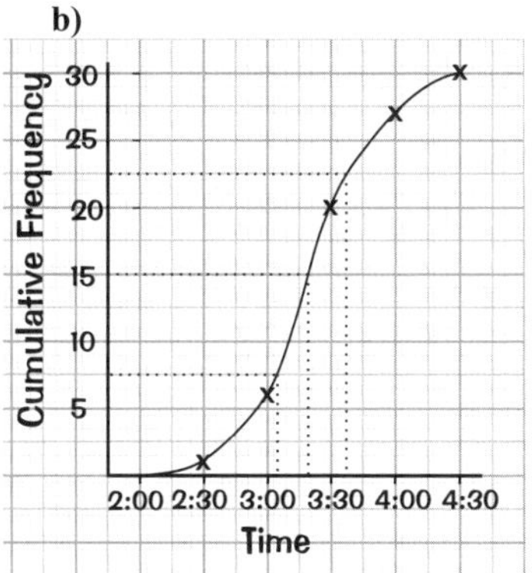

c) median = 3:19 (±3)
upper quartile = 3:37 (±3)
lower quartile = 3:05 (±3)

d) 0:32 (±5)

Pages 123-124 — Histograms and Frequency Density

Q1 4 × 10 = 40 people

Q2

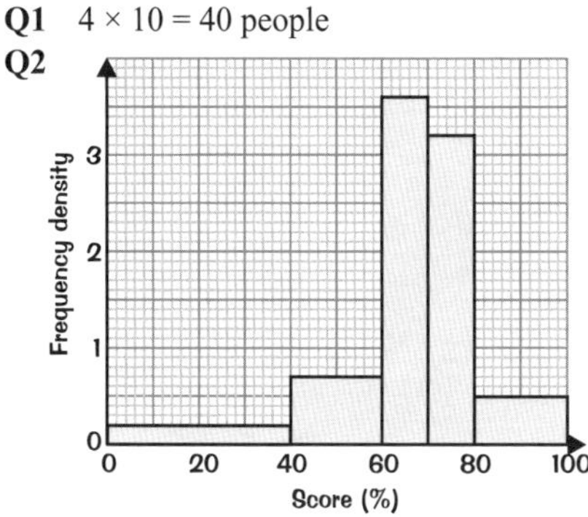

Q3 a) Frequency for $150 < x \leqslant 200 = 275$

b)

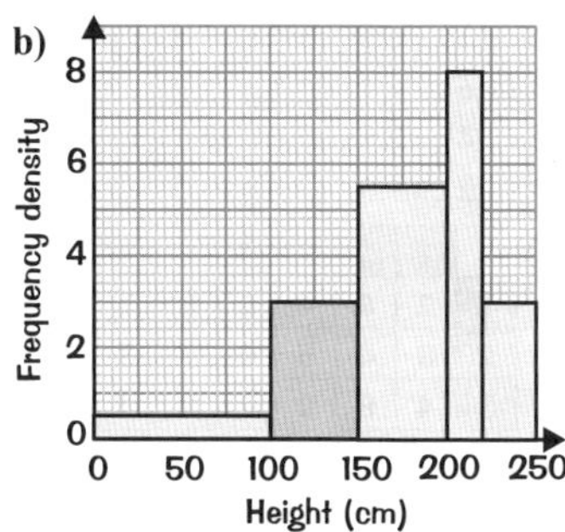

Q4 a)

Weight (kg)	0≤w<2	2≤w<4	4≤w<7	7≤w<9	9≤w<15
Frequency	3	2	6	9	12
Frequency density	1.5	1	2	4.5	2

b)

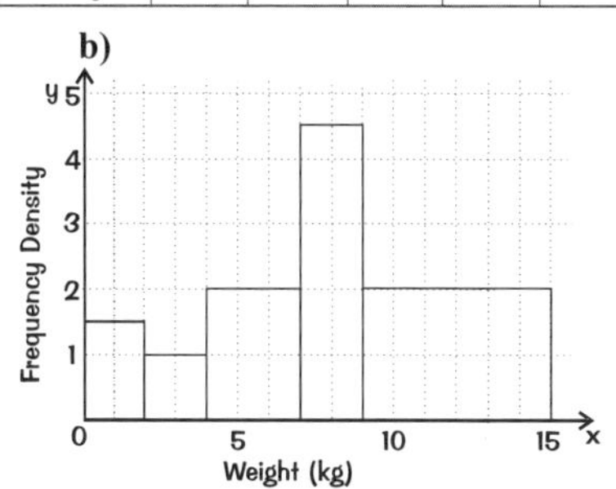

c) 23 hives

Q5 a)

Salary (£1000s)	0 ≤ s < 10	10 ≤ s < 20	20 ≤ s < 30	30 ≤ s < 40	40 ≤ s < 50
Frequency	10	25	42	20	3
Frequency Density	1	2.5	4.2	2	0.3

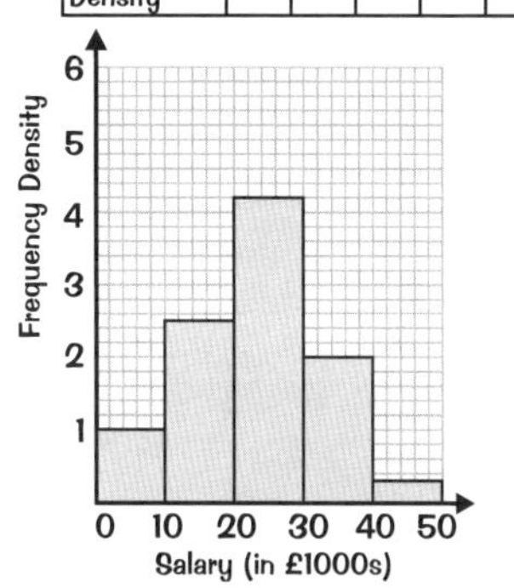

b) E.g. there are more people with higher salaries now than 10 years ago.

Q6 a)

Milk (litres)	Frequency	Frequency density	Mid-interval	Frequency × mid-interval
0≤C<1	6	6	0.5	3
1≤C<5	6	1.5	3	18
5≤C<8	6	2	6.5	39
8≤C<10	6	3	9	54
10≤C<15	6	1.2	12.5	75
15≤C<20	6	1.2	17.5	105

b) 8.2 litres (to 1 d.p.)

c)

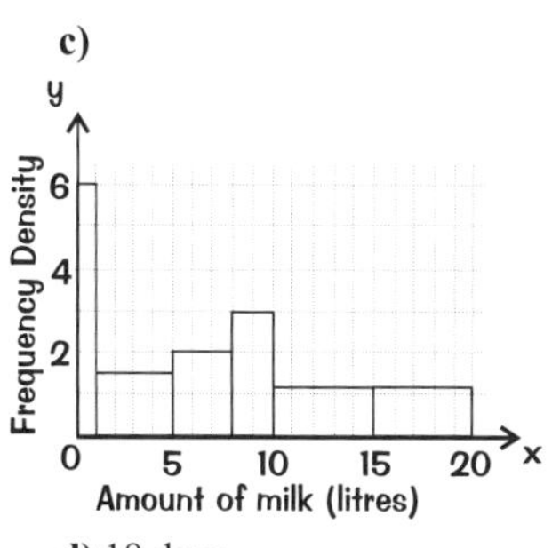

d) 18 days

Pages 125-127 — Other Graphs and Charts

Q1 $\frac{360°}{100} = 3.6°$ per gram

Carbohydrate	3.6 × 35 = 126°
Protein	3.6 × 15 = 54°
Fat	3.6 × 10 = 36°
Magical Fairy Dust	3.6 × 40 = 144°
	360°

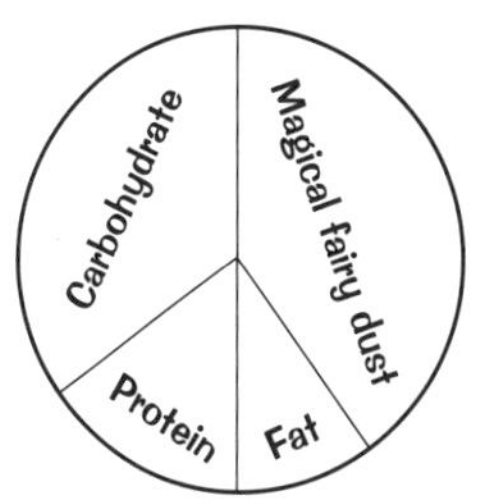

Q2 Sherrington 380,000 = 148° (approx)
2600 visitors = 1°
So, to the nearest 10,000:
Brompton = 2600 × 118° ≈ 310,000
Barny = 2600 × 44° ≈ 110,000
Livsea = 2600 × 50° ≈ 130,000

Q3 c)

Q4 It's not possible to tell whether more people voted for the Green Party in 2009, because you can't tell how many people voted in either election.

Q5 a) 60 b) 8 c) 4
d) e.g. Cola was the most popular and milk the least popular / cola was much more popular than milk.

Q6 a) Monday, Wednesday and Thursday.
b) Monday

Q7 a) 60% b) About 10%

Q8

	Van	Motor-bike	Car	Total
Travelling North	15	12	21	48
Travelling South	20	9	23	52
Total	35	21	44	100

a) 35 c) 9
b) 52 d) 21

Q9 a)

	Wings	No wings	Total
Antennae	6	4	10
No antennae	6	9	15
Total	12	13	25

b) 9
c) 25

1019 - 19730

Answers: P128 — P132

Pages 128-132 — Probability

Q1 **a)** 1/2 **c)** 1/6
b) 2/3 **d)** 0
And so should be arranged approximately like this on the number line.

Guatemalan stamp — 0; Five on a dice; Head on a coin — 0.5; Red ball; 1

Q2 Debbie's chance of winning would be 1/9. This is greater than 0.1, so she would choose to play.

Q3 The probability of a head is still 1/2

Q4 1 – 0.27 = 0.73 or 73/100

Q5 **a)** 5/12 **c)** 3/12 = 1/4
b) 4/12 = 1/3 **d)** 9/12 = 3/4

Q6 **a)** 40/132 = 10/33
b) P(car being blue or green) = 45/132
P(not blue or green) = 87/132
= 29/44

Q7

	1	2	3	4	5
1	1,1	1,2	1,3	1,4	1,5
2	2,1	2,2	2,3	2,4	2,5
3	3,1	3,2	3,3	3,4	3,5
4	4,1	4,2	4,3	4,4	4,5
5	5,1	5,2	5,3	5,4	5,5
6	6,1	6,2	6,3	6,4	6,5

Q8 **a)**

Outcome	Frequency
W	8
D	5
L	7

b) The 3 outcomes are not equally likely.
c) 1/4
d) They are most likely to win.
e) 14

Q9 **a)** $\frac{1}{13}$ **b)** $\frac{2}{39}$ **c)** $\frac{1}{36}$

Q10 **a)** $\frac{7}{12}$ **b)** $\frac{7}{12}$
c) The two events can both happen at the same time, since 3 is a white.

Q11 **a)** $\frac{2}{5}$ **b)** $\frac{4}{15}$ **c)** $\frac{2}{3}$

Q12 **a)** (1,1), (1,2), (1,3), (1,4), (1,5), (1,6), (1,7), (2,1), (2,2), (2,3), (2,4), (2,5), (2,6), (2,7), (3,1), (3,2), (3,3), (3,4), (3,5), (3,6), (3,7)

b)

	1	2	3	4	5	6	7
1	2	3	4	5	6	7	8
2	3	4	5	6	7	8	9
3	4	5	6	7	8	9	10

c) $\frac{1}{7}$ **d)** $\frac{11}{21}$
e) $\frac{2}{7}$ **f)** $\frac{5}{7}$
g) Subtract the answer to part **e)** from 1.

Q13 **a)**

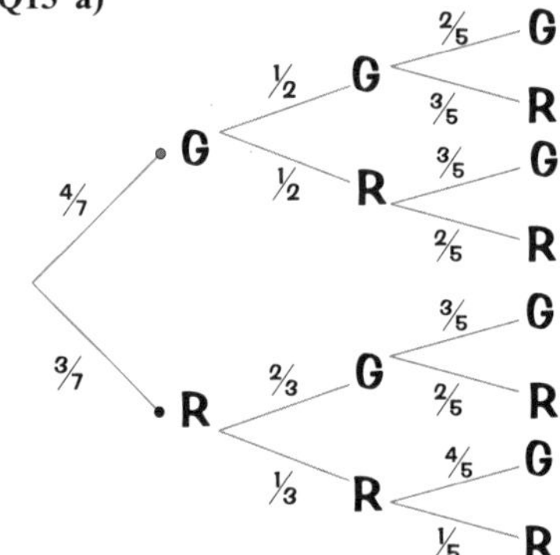

b) $\frac{18}{35}$
c) $\frac{3}{7}$

Q14 **a)** 14/40 or 0.35
b) 24/60 = 0.4
c) 38/100 = 0.38

Q15 4 times

Q16

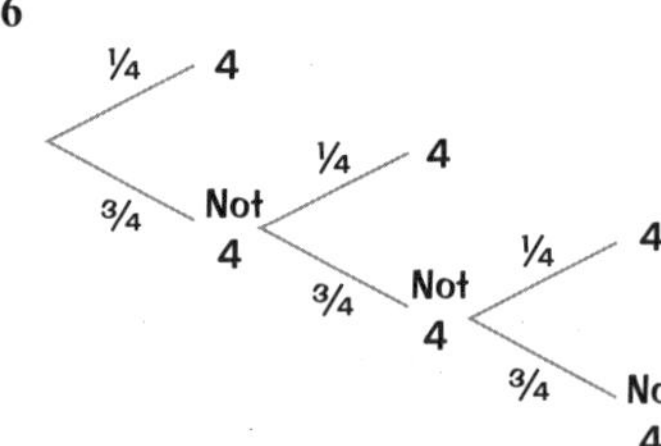

a) $\frac{3}{16}$ **b)** $\frac{37}{64}$

Q17 **a)**

7/11 £: 3/5 £ (5/9 £, 4/9 20p); 2/5 20p (2/3 £, 1/3 20p)
4/11 20p: 7/10 £ (2/3 £, 1/3 20p); 3/10 20p (7/9 £, 2/9 20p)

b) $\frac{28}{55}$ **c)** $\frac{46}{165}$

Q18 **a)** $\frac{1}{4}$
b) $\frac{1}{2}$ **c)** $\frac{1}{2}$

Q19 $\frac{1}{28}$

Q20 **a)**

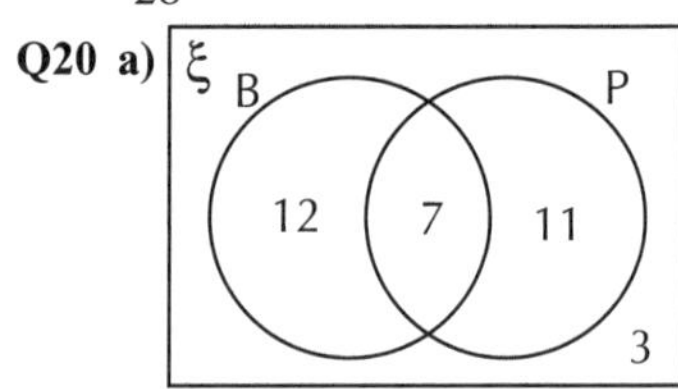

b) i) $\frac{19}{33}$
ii) $\frac{15}{33} = \frac{5}{11}$

Q21 **a)**

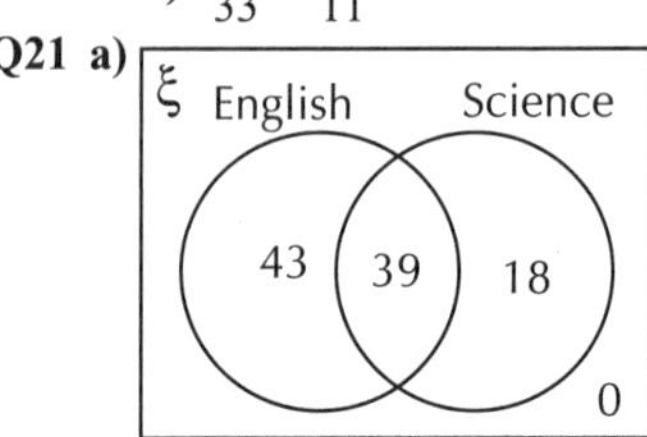

b) $\frac{39}{57} = \frac{13}{19}$

Q22 **a)** $x^2 + 2x + 22 = 121$
So $x^2 + 2x - 99 = 0$
i.e. $(x + 11)(x - 9) = 0$
This means $x = 9$.
b) $\frac{22}{121} = \frac{2}{11}$
c) $\frac{2}{7}$

ISBN 978 1 78294 673 1
9 781782 946731
MEAI43

£2.00
(Retail Price)